dangerous territory

MY MISGUIDED QUEST
TO SAVE THE WORLD

AMY PETERSON

Discovery House.

Discovery House is affiliated with Our Daily Bread Ministries, Grand Rapids, Michigan.

Requests for permission to quote from this book should be directed to: Permissions Department, Discovery House, P.O. Box 3566, Grand Rapids, MI 49501, or contact us by e-mail at permissionsdept@dhp.org.

Scripture quotations on pages 43, 170, 177, and 191 are from The Holy Bible, English Standard Version® (ESV®), copyright © 2001 by Crossway, a publishing ministry of Good News Publishers. Used by permission. All rights reserved.

Scripture quotation on page 74 is from the HOLY BIBLE: EASY-TO-READ VERSION © 2001 by World Bible Translation Center, Inc. and is used by permission.

Scripture quotations on pages 75, 121, 182, 192, and 212 are from the Holy Bible, New International Version®, NIV®. Copyright © 1973, 1978, 1984, 2011 by Biblica, Inc.™ Used by permission of Zondervan. All rights reserved worldwide. www.zondervan.com. The "NIV" and "New International Version" are trademarks registered in the United States Patent and Trademark Office by Biblica, Inc.™

Scripture quotation on page 112 is from the New American Standard Bible®, copyright © 1960, 1962, 1963, 1968, 1971, 1972, 1973, 1975, 1977, 1995 by The Lockman Foundation. Used by permission. (www.Lockman.org)

Scripture quotation on page 194 is from the Amplified® Bible, copyright © 1954, 1958, 1962, 1964, 1965, 1987 by The Lockman Foundation. Used by permission.

Excerpt from "Journey of the Magi" from *Collected Poems, 1909–1962* by T. S. Eliot. Copyright 1936 by Houghton Mifflin Harcourt Publishing Company. Copyright © renewed 1964 by Thomas Stearns Eliot. Reprinted by permission of Houghton Mifflin Harcourt Publishing Company. All rights reserved.

Permission to quote "The Greatest" by Chan Marshall/Cat Power (2006) granted by Mattitude Music LLC.

Permission to quote "Clam, Crab, Cockle, Cowrie" (2004) granted by Joanna Newsom.

Library of Congress Cataloging-in-Publication Data

Names: Peterson, Amy (Assistant Director of Honors Programming at Taylor University), author.
Title: Dangerous territory : my misguided quest to save the world / Amy Peterson.
Description: Grand Rapids : Discovery House, 2017.
Identifiers: LCCN 2016046651 | ISBN 9781627075978
Subjects: LCSH: Peterson, Amy (Assistant Director of Honors Programming at Taylor University),
    author. | Missionaries--United States--Biography. | Missions.
Classification: LCC BV3705.P47 A3 2017 | DDC 266.0092 [B] --dc23
LC record available at https://lccn.loc.gov/2016046651

Printed in the United States of America
First printing in 2017

For Rosemary and Owen,
for Veronica,
and for you:
bright with hope,
bruised reed,
beloved.

Contents

A Note on Memoir

Memory offers us a partial and imperfect view of the past, one that is often self-serving. In writing about events that took place over a decade ago, I have tried to be honest, relying heavily on my journals. But even journals provide no guarantee of an accurate depiction, as they too offer only my perspective—no one else's. In this book, I have changed most of the names, and in a case or two I have conflated a few friends into a single character for the sake of simplicity in the storyline, but other than that, all of these stories are true: this is the world as best as I can remember it.

Yet she could see by their shocked and altered faces
that even their virtues were being burned away.

Flannery O'Connor

All this was a long time ago, I remember,
And I would do it again, but set down
This set down
This: were we led all that way for
Birth or Death? There was a Birth, certainly,
We had evidence and no doubt. I had seen birth and death,
But had thought they were different; this Birth was
Hard and bitter agony for us, like Death, our death.
We returned to our place, these Kingdoms,
But no longer at ease here, in the old dispensation,
With an alien people clutching their gods.
I should be glad of another death.

from "Journey of the Magi" by T. S. Eliot

Introduction

Dear Young Reader,

This book was written for people like you, young men and women who want their lives to make a difference. The complaint of many young people today is, "I'm so bored." One thing we can promise you: If you give your life fully to Jesus Christ, you will never lack for adventure! . . .

You're probably being pushed by somebody to take some kind of dare. Okay, we dare you, too. We dare you to pray, "Lord, make my life count," and see what happens!

from *Heaven's Heroes: Real Life Stories from History's Greatest Missionaries* by David Shibley (1989)

Dear Reader,

I wanted to be extraordinary, the greatest, truest kind of Christian, one whose life *counted*—not one who raised 2.5 children behind a white picket fence in American suburbia. I wanted to be one of heaven's heroes.

But after two years in Southeast Asia, I moved to the foothills of Southern California. I took an office job and spent my weekends hiking in the San Gabriels or lying on Newport Beach. My fiancé gave me a CD by Cat Power, and I listened to Chan Marshall's lush melodies and haunting piano over and over as I drove down the Orange Freeway to work.

> Once I wanted to be the greatest
> No wind or waterfall could stall me

And then came the rush of the flood
The stars at night turned deep to dust

Melt me down.

I didn't cry anymore when I listened, just watched the sun move across the foothills and felt something shift inside me, something soften and relax, like exhaling after holding my breath for years and years.

This is the story of how I was melted down.

PART ONE

• • • • • • • • • •

SENT

Expect great things from God; attempt great things for God.

William Carey

1

. . . . .

I Can't Tell You This Country's Name

I longed to be a martyr, to be one of that "noble army." . . . I longed to do something. I had a strong desire to be a missionary, to give myself up to some holy work, and I had a firm belief that such a calling would be mine.

Ann Martin Hinderer, missionary to West Africa

Far too large a proportion of people [who are applying for missionary work] are seriously pathological.

a member of the Committee for Women's Work, 1915

I gravitated toward her because she was the only one in the room who looked like me: too young to be there, the confidence of the clueless tossed like a mantle over her shoulders, dreamy idealism shining in her eyes. Both blond and twenty-two years old, Rebekah and I stood out in the group of grad students gathered for the welcome dinner for our low-residency master's program. Most of the others were older and experienced, having just returned from a year or more of teaching English in Asia. They clustered in knots, the group with greasy hair and flowy clothes using exotic words like *mabu*

dofu and *joudza*, the scrubbed and modestly buttoned-up ones diligently discussing textbooks and area churches.

Watching them, I remembered what I'd overheard in the campus bookstore that morning. The manager, training a new sales clerk, had warned her: "Watch out for those folk in class this month. They're a little kooky." *Kooky* might not have been the word I'd have chosen, but as I sat down next to Rebekah, I wondered if this was my future: Would I become one of the strange ones? They didn't glow with holiness the way I expected missionaries to: instead, they seemed like they might have chosen to live overseas because they never quite fit in America.

"Hey," said Adam, laying his paper plate of pizza on the table next to me. "Can I sit here?"

We were three skinny new kids, fresh-faced, wide-eyed and shivering in the air-conditioning of the basement classroom, fingering garlic bread and cans of Coke. We weren't cowering, exactly. We were watching, trying to figure out what moving to Asia to teach English was going to be like, how it was going to change us. We chewed pizza slowly and observed.

• • •

I had developed a set of answers I gave when people asked what I was doing after college.

When my women's lit professor Dr. Matthews asked, I gave the short answer. "I'm moving to Southeast Asia to teach English as a Second Language at a university," I said. "I'll also be doing a master's program in intercultural studies."

This answer was good, especially for my academic friends. It sounded legitimate. And it neatly avoided the word *missionary*.

Despite my sincere and passionate desire to change the world for God, I hated that term—*missionary*—for all the connotations and baggage trailing behind it. I dreaded being aligned with the long history of abuse that educated westerners commonly associated with "missions"—destruction of indigenous cultures in the name of Christ, introduction of foreign diseases, wars in the name of evangelism. If I had told Dr. Matthews that I was going to be a missionary, she would have thought of Nathan Price. The patriarch in Barbara Kingsolver's novel *The Poisonwood Bible*, Price stood for the culturally blind failures of modern missions. He tried to baptize new Congolese converts in a river filled with crocodiles. He proclaimed "*Tata Jesus is bangala!*" thinking he was saying, "Jesus is beloved," when in fact the phrase meant "Jesus is

poisonwood." Despite being corrected many times, Price repeated the phrase until his death.

I knew enough to recognize that Nathan Price did not represent all missionaries, and there were many I admired. But I also knew enough to be embarrassed. I knew that the British had used "protecting missionaries" as an excuse for imperial expansion in India and China. I knew that some of the early Franciscan missionaries had been unequivocally committed to Spanish imperialism, even condoning the violence and forced conversions of the Conquest. I knew that in the Americas, Christian evangelism was nearly without exception the primary logic used by "reformers" who set up boarding schools for native children, forcing them away from their homes and traditions.

It wasn't just that I feared what Dr. Matthews and others would think of me. I was terrified that I might accidentally live into this horrific, ethnocentric, imperialistic tradition.

I didn't even use the word *missionary* in my second standard answer. This one was for my parents' friends and people at church in Arkansas. When, over donuts and coffee in the foyer on Sunday mornings, they asked what I would be doing after college, I'd say that I was going to teach English in Southeast Asia. "Oh, like for missions?" they'd ask, southern drawls drawing out the words.

"Well, yeah, but the country isn't open to missionaries. I'm just going to be a Christian English teacher," I'd reply. I liked to say that I was going to live my life with God in a foreign country. I planned to be a Christian in my new home, teach ESL there to the best of my ability, and practice loving God and loving the people around me. In fact, I chose my sending organization because they described their goals in this way—they didn't use the word *missions* either.

I couldn't have explained to people at church my reservations about becoming one of the photographs pinned on the church missions board. I couldn't have explained that I was relieved to be going to a "closed" country, where evangelism was technically forbidden, because in some unspoken way I wasn't fully convinced that the Message I was bringing was strong to save, or that it was even truly true. I disliked the idea of cold evangelism, so I was glad to be teaching in a place where my main goal could be simpler, just to be a faithful presence and to provide a desired service—language lessons.

But of course, regardless of whether or not I used the word, I *was* a missionary; I sent out letters asking for prayers and money, and gave people refrigerator magnets of my face. The suitcase I would carry across the ocean

didn't hold my own clothes; it held clothes I had bought for someone playing the mythic role of a "missionary"—long skirts, loose linen pants, sensible brown shoes. And when I explained to my supporters my decision to go, I said as much. I still didn't use the word, but I asked for what we all called "fruit": I asked them to pray that I would find girls to disciple in my new home.

• • •

"Where are you going?" Adam asked Rebekah, while gathering our paper plates for the trashcan. They, like most of our classmates, were headed to China. I wasn't. Even now, a decade later, I can't tell you the name of the country where I worked. My students and friends, whose names have been changed in this book, remain under police surveillance because of the story I'm about to tell you, because of everything that happened while I was there. I told Rebekah and Adam where I was going, but that I didn't know yet what city I'd be in. Camille, our country director, would update me as soon as my placement was finalized.

"What made you decide to go?" Rebekah asked me. Having heard her and Adam talk, I knew that these were people who could be trusted with the whole story, the long answer I was still trying to work out, the one that was as honest about my evangelical zeal as it was about my hesitations.

"I grew up reading missionary biographies," I began, certain Rebekah would understand, that she had found her glow in the same evangelical world I had. I'd grown up believing that the most important, most spiritual, Christians were the pastors and missionaries. I was taught that as a woman I couldn't be a pastor, but I preferred the missionary path anyway—pastoring sounded like it could be boring, but missions was sure to be full of adventure, exotic destinations, and wild experiences.

As a child, I wanted to be like Amy Carmichael, who had redefined what kind of work was possible for a single woman in 1800s Ireland by starting a Bible study for poor young women who worked at the mills. Soon over five hundred women attended weekly. Later, she spent fifty years in India, assimilating into the native culture. She snuck into temples and rescued child prostitutes.

The glamorous, glorious stories of people like Amy Carmichael, Hudson Taylor, Gladys Aylward, George Müller, and Jim Elliot shaped my imagination in my formative years, and I believed that the most valuable way I could serve God was to serve God overseas.

Sure, if you had asked me, I would have said there was no division be-tween "sacred" and "secular" work—that copy editing at a publishing house could be just as meaningful and worthwhile as moving to a foreign land for God—but I didn't really believe it. How could I? No one wrote biographies of housewives. Accountants never snuck into temples. Copy editors never changed the world.

Sermons about lives of full dedication to God rarely made daily floor-sweeping an example of dedication. They seldom lauded people who re-sponded to e-mails punctually and thoughtfully. They didn't praise those who regularly attended conferences for professional development and stayed up-to-date in their fields.

I wanted an extraordinary life, flush with spiritual vitality and adventure, a life fully committed to God. I wanted to be the greatest.

"And when I was a teenager, I promised God that I would spend a year overseas either before, during, or after college," I continued. I'd been on a youth group retreat. Fifty or sixty of us sun-kissed, leggy teens, slapping mosquitoes away at dusk, listening to our pastor speak, infusing us with what he called God's vision for the world. Of course at the end he asked us, with every head bowed and every eye closed, to raise a hand as a pledge that we would spend at least one year serving God overseas. ("Mormon youth spend two years doing missionary work! Don't you think you can give God one?" he pushed.) I didn't feel pressure, though. I didn't do it to please the pastor. I raised my hand because I felt, even at sixteen, that it was nearly inevitable: I knew in my bones that I would be leaving.

"Did you go to OneDay?" I asked, pausing.

"No. I went to Urbana twice, though," Rebekah said. Urbana was the biggest annual missions conference aimed at mobilizing college-aged people into overseas service. I told her about OneDay.

The summer after our freshman year, my friends and I had road-tripped to Shelby Farms outside Memphis for the event. We camped in a large, flat field with thousands of other college students, gathering before a stage early in the morning, kneeling in groups and praying. When the music began, with insistent thrumming bass lines and driving guitar, we stood and lifted our hands. Our bodies swayed with passion, our Chacos drummed the ground, we lay flat on our faces in the damp dirt and wept.

Later we sat, bandanas wrapped around our greasy braids, prayer journals opened and pens held ready, listening to John Piper. Nodding, we agreed with him that our lives would not be organized around 401ks and retirement funds. Our eyes shone as we rejected the American dream that led to a safe

suburban existence, golden years aimed toward golf courses. Rapt, we could almost see the example he gave us as an alternative, a story from his church. Two widows in their sixties had moved to Africa, and spent years serving there. One day, driving a jeep down a mountain, their brakes went out and the car flew off a cliff, "soaring into eternity," Piper said, gazing into the clouds as if the women might still be up there, flying above us now.

I imagined them, gray haired Minnesotan ladies, but like Thelma and Louise, finally free. That had to have been a more meaningful life than they could have had in America, leading quilting groups and prayer circles, baking cookies for their grandchildren, organizing church rummage sales. Golfing.

I wanted that more meaningful life. I wanted the adventures that I had been promised, and I couldn't see any way for a woman to have them except on the mission field.

A few years later, I'd met a famous missionary. She was back in the States after three months of imprisonment by the Taliban for preaching the gospel in an Islamic state. She put her hand on my shoulder, looked into my eyes, and said softly that she felt God had chosen me for something special. My heart warmed. I wanted so badly to believe her.

Despite all the cautious posturing of my standard answers, the truth was that I wanted to save the world. My reasonable explanations about university teaching and living life with God in a foreign place masked a deep zeal to do big things, to make a difference. My educated, cynical view of the history of missions was simply a veneer overlaying an evangelistic passion instilled from childhood. I was a conflicted missionary—desperate to save the world and afraid of doing it wrong—but also very willing just to go love God in a new place. I was equal parts zeal for God's glory, hunger for adventure, and fear of failure.

Rebekah and Adam understood. As our other classmates joined the conversation, I realized that I was happy to be part of a kind-of-weird group of people. After all, I wrote in my journal later that night, weren't we supposed to be strangers and aliens on earth?

• • •

Rebekah and I bonded over our newness, and during study dates at Borders, I told her about my sort-of-ex-boyfriend, Charley, with his floppy brown hair and crooked smile. We'd broken up a year earlier, but despite the misogynistic undertones to his theology I still thought maybe I loved him. We weren't

exactly together, though as it turned out, he was moving to Asia to teach English too. Maybe that was a sign? Rebekah wasn't convinced.

"Can you see yourself marrying him?" she asked. I stuck a pen in my textbook and folded it closed, chewing my bottom lip.

"I don't know. I don't know if I even want to be married," I admitted.

Charley and I had had a troubled relationship, off and on and off again. Perhaps I simply wasn't ready to settle down, or commit. I wanted to be free to go.

Halfway through our intensive classes, I still didn't know exactly where I'd be going. Maybe the slow and complicated nature of my city placement should have been a warning of what was to come, of the fact that there were multiple powers at play in the region and that not all of them welcomed foreign influence—but at the time I just assumed delays were par for the course in international work.

Finally, in mid-July, Camille sat down next to me at the cafeteria table, pulling a blue cardigan over her shoulders. The air-conditioner ran at full blast; we were constantly moving from freezing classrooms to heat-saturated sidewalks and back again. I liked Camille, but found her intimidating: there was a solidity to her, something that said she would not be moved. Later that characteristic would be comforting, but when I first met her, I always felt naïve and tongue-tied in her presence.

"We have a placement." Camille smiled a brittle and shaded smile, like a teacher announcing an exam to an untested pupil. Streaks of the noon sun through the skylight lit our plastic food trays. I pushed mine back as she opened her laptop and edged it into a patch of shade.

"Here's your city." Camille pointed to a map dot near the coast in the center of the country.

"Great!" I said happily, wondering why her smile seemed tempered. Was there sadness in her eyes, or uncertainty? "We've only had teachers there for one year," she continued. Her piercing blue eyes made contact with mine. "Both of them have returned to the States now, so you will be placed there with another new teacher, Lisa. We don't know of any other foreigners in the city . . . or any Christians or churches. It's a very poor area, too—still suffering from the devastation of wars."

My excitement was undiminished. Camille paused before going on, wanting to make sure my expectations were adjusted appropriately. "This is a hard place," she said finally. "It's hard soil. Over the last year, we haven't seen any spiritual interest."

"Okay," I said, not sure what reaction she wanted from me. "That's fine. I'm just glad to know where I'm going next month." In truth, it was exactly

what I would have chosen for myself: the hardest place, the most unreached, the farthest-flung and most adventurous, was the place I wanted to be.

Later that week, I journaled on my laptop:

How do I find the balance—I don't want to treat people like objects, like items on a conversion checklist. I don't want to have the attitude of a self-righteous crusader going to save the heathen. I just want to go live my life for God in a place where he is not known.

But I don't want the simplicity of that attitude to lead to my developing a "small" view of what God can accomplish. Too many people I know seem to have settled with low expectations for their overseas work. They seem resigned.

How can I learn to expect big things of God without thinking big things about myself?

Like a good Christian girl, I wrote to the people who were supporting me with their prayers and their dollars. I told them about my city placement, and I asked them to pray. I asked them to pray that by the end of my year there, I would have two or three girls to disciple.

Unlike a good Christian girl, I didn't really expect God to answer.

• • •

"I just don't see you with Charley," Rebekah said as we entered a lamplit hotel ballroom. We were in California now, for just a few days of teacher training before flying out.

"I see you more with someone like . . . him." She pointed across the room, past a hundred or more nascent English teachers, to a man standing quietly against the wall, hands in his pockets. He wore a plaid button-down in earth tones, one that looked fresh from Goodwill, with grey slacks and tennis shoes. Slender and tall, his brown hair curled gently across his forehead above wire-rim glasses. He was totally adorable.

"Jack?" I'd met him, briefly. He was headed to the same country I was. "Yeah, he's okay, I guess," I said. Rebekah and I sat on padded chairs near the back, and I watched Jack. Two exuberant girls rushed over to him. One touched his arm, the other rolling her eyes and laughing as she told a story, and they pulled him to a seat.

"Hey," Charley said, grabbing the chair next to mine. The same organization that was sending me to Southeast Asia was arranging his placement at a university in China.

"Hey," I smiled, squeezing his hand. He looked good in his blue button-down. "How's it going?"

"Good," he said. "Our group is actually meeting in the other ballroom for most of these sessions, so I can't stay. But I'll look for you later," he said, his voice rising at the end, asking.

"Yeah," I said. "Sounds good."

• • •

Several days later, our plane left at two in the morning. As it rose over the dark Pacific Ocean, I wondered if I should feel regret about the night before: Charley and I had kissed again. We had broken up so many times, but never managed to make it a good, clean break. I kept coming back to him, craving the way he comforted and companioned me, but we each had too many edges that didn't fit, and we just ended up frustrating each other. Facing such a drastic transition, I had wanted something to hold on to; selfishly, perhaps, I had wanted the comfort of his presence, the familiarity of his kiss.

But in the airplane, under my blanket, trying to sleep, my thoughts drifted easily away from Charley, an indication, maybe, of where my heart truly was. I was thinking about leaving Rebekah and my new grad school friends, who already felt like best friends. I was thinking about LAX. We had boarded at one in the morning, and the terminal had been packed with people. Few of the faces in the crowded seats and aisles had been white. An Indian woman in a crimson sari had slept beautifully, dangled across one seat. Chinese children had played with crayons on the floor. Exhaustion and hopelessness crept across the faces of those who still had hours to wait.

When we had checked our bags, two Asian women at the desk were attempting, with little English, to check in too. They had no tickets. An experienced teacher had stepped in to help translate.

As I fell into a light sleep on the airplane, high above the Pacific, I imagined that someday, I could be that person—the one who translates, the one who helps people get tickets home.

Interlude

There is a structure that this story is supposed to follow. First, the childhood—protected or troubled, innocent or complicated. Early signs of unusual holiness, or a youth misspent. A conversion. An encounter. A calling. A commitment to go, against all odds, against the advice of family and friends, despite any health concerns, regardless of the cultural norms she is bucking, willingly surrendering any romantic interests. Once across the ocean, there are difficulties, but they are always overcome by faith and prayer. There are miracles. Sometimes there is tragedy: children die, love is denied, people (sometimes including our hero) are imprisoned. These tragedies fade by the end of the story, though, and the hero fairly beams with the glory of God. Her story lacks complexity: there are good characters, and evil; there is right and there is wrong. Her everyday activities are imbued with more purpose and meaning than ours are, back home; she is the rugged individual off to save the world.

We do not ask what happened when the converts were rejected by their families. We do not ask what happened to the young wife who rarely saw her missionary husband, to the children he only kissed once before dying in the concentration camp. We do not ask who cared for her parents while she was across the ocean. We skip the part where he died of grief after the missionary children were killed. We do not know if they doubted God. We do not wonder why all our protagonists are white.

We do not want the story to be too real.

This missionary narrative, the one found in almost every biography I read growing up, came into its own thanks to Jonathan Edwards, the Puritan preacher and theologian perhaps best known for his sermon "Sinners in the Hands of an Angry God." Edwards was a friend of David Brainerd, who spent three years attempting to evangelize Native American tribes in the 1740s. After Brainerd's death, Edwards edited and published his friend's diaries, transforming him from an obscure, sickly, and largely ineffectual missionary into a saintly folk hero who embodied authentic spirituality and sacrificed his life for the cause of Christ. America fell in love with the story: an orphaned young man who heard a call from God went to Yale, faced "persecution" there, devoted his life to missions, fell sick after only a few years, and died in the arms of his betrothed—Edwards's daughter Jerusha.

The romanticized *Life of David Brainerd* was the most popular of all Edwards's works. Brainerd became a legendary character: a frontier saint who lived on bear meat and Indian corn meal, who regularly slept on the hard ground. When he encountered poisonous snakes, the stories said, those snakes refused to bite him. He spent so long in prayer, knees bent and hands clasped, that afterward he was unable to walk or flex his fingers.

In 1810 the American Board of Commissioners for Foreign Missions was formed, and the first generation of American missionaries was sent across the oceans. Many of them had been inspired to serve by Edwards's book, and when they wrote their own stories, they followed its example. The story was an epic Christian journey—a pilgrimage, a quest for spiritual knowledge and experience as well as for converts. There was a ritualistic separation from family, friends, and home followed by physical and spiritual tests. The missionary experience was a rite of passage into evangelical adulthood, and eventually into the missionary hall of fame.

We might say that with *The Life of David Brainerd*, Jonathan Edwards created the American "missionary myth." Calling it a myth doesn't mean it's a lie, only that it became iconic and, through repetition, came to symbolize our deepest convictions about morality and the nature of reality. Our evangelical missionary myth grew up alongside the American myth of the frontier hero: in each, a rugged individual is off to conquer a new land for the good of a community. The missionary was a heroic and determined individual, someone special and set apart.

So far I'm failing to fit my own story into the narrative mold: I've told you little of my childhood, and nothing of my conversion. You've seen how conflicted I am about my "calling" to missions.

Let us see if I can do better as we go on.

2
· · · · ·

Backpackers and Wanderlust

My soul longs to feel itself more of a pilgrim and stranger here below, that nothing may divert me from pressing through the lonely desert, till I arrive at my Father's house.

David Brainerd

What might it not mean for others if all of us who are seeking after a country of our own, a better Country, that is, a heavenly, lived more like pilgrims here?

Amy Carmichael, *Gold Cord*

The country director, Camille, met us at the airport with a case of bottled water and a fifteen-passenger van. Lisa and I helped each other lift our suitcases into the back, and then I slid down a sun-baked bench seat toward the window, trying to memorize everything I saw. The drive into the capital was a study in contrasts: new electronics factories on one side of the road; shacks selling bottles of Coke and Fanta on the other. Rice fields and water buffalo on my left; slender, three-story colonial buildings in pastel colors on my right. I jotted down notes for a letter home to Grandma, who didn't have e-mail and would expect handwritten updates.

Grandma hadn't been thrilled that I was moving overseas. Mostly, she was worried I would end up marrying a foreigner. Her concern didn't stop her from supporting me; along with money she gave me plenty of advice. In truth, I thought Grandma, of all people—the woman who took me to Scotland when I was fifteen, the one who regularly traveled around the world—would understand at least one of the reasons I wanted to go. I thought she also had a touch of the wanderer in her.

Grandma liked to tell stories about her mother, Nellie, who grew up on a Colorado ranch at the turn of the century. Nellie's parents divorced when her mother told her father, "It's the race horse or me. Choose." Her dad moved west, to Salt Lake City. When Nellie graduated from high school, she packed a single suitcase and hopped the first train to visit her father. Together, the two of them traveled down the west coast, from Alaska to Glendora, California, working odd jobs, living in logging camps, seeing the country.

I say Grandma liked to tell that story, but really, I always asked for it— because in Nellie I glimpsed some genetic excuse for my wanderlust, some hereditary reason for the fact that most of my dreams involved buses, trains, and backpacks.

Maybe it's part of a mythical American heritage for those of us descended from immigrant and pioneer stock, those who left Europe dirt poor, the ones who never stopped searching for a new frontier. We sing about "wide open spaces" and riding off on trains "to look for America." We believe that leaving holds some answer.

At the age of twenty-two, I'd already lived in six cities and traveled to twelve countries. My senior thesis in college had been about this mythic ideal of wanderlust in American pop culture. When I decided to move overseas, it hadn't felt like a sacrifice—it had felt like a rite of passage. Sure, I'd be far from my family, unable to stay up to date on movies or purchase a Frappuccino or wear a two-piece at the beach or browse in an English bookstore. But honestly, I thought people should be jealous of me, not pitying me.

I even viewed it as a Christian virtue, this willingness to leave, to lead an uncomfortable and migratory existence. It's what God called Abraham to do, after all—to leave his home and travel to an unknown destination. I treasured my wanderlust, seeing it as part of my desire to live a meaningful life rather than one organized around personal comfort.

I didn't want avoiding discomfort to become one of my life goals. I'd seen too many Americans live that way, and it ended in suburban homes with two-car garages and lots of television to mask the ennui. I wanted a less comfortable life, one where I didn't feel poured into a snug, safe, preexisting mold.

I got to go. I got to leave. I had found a new frontier. This was the American dream. And I got to do it in the name of God. Suddenly my fear of commitment took on a nice religious sheen. Going was the righteous thing to do.

At the outskirts of the capital, traffic thickened and slowed. Scooters and bikes zipped around us, honking madly to announce their presence, ignoring the suggestions made by traffic lights. Women with long hair in low ponytails swept the sidewalks and stoked fires in small curbside grills, turning kabobs over the flames. Motorbike taxi drivers lounged on their stationary machines, clustered at street corners, smoking cigarettes and pulling on hats to protect against the sun. The air-conditioning in our van blew full force on my face. I reached up to close the vent, allowing myself to feel the heat.

• • •

All the English teachers spent five days training in the capital, beginning every day with breakfast at six. I'd come down from the shoebox of a hotel room I shared with another teacher, through the lobby that smelled of boiled eggs and perfumed cleaning fluids, to a plentiful Continental breakfast. There were bread and eggs plus all kinds of new things: rice porridge, mango juice, dragon fruit with its gorgeous pink-petaled skin and white flesh flecked with black. Instrumental versions of American pop songs from the sixties and seventies played softly over the speakers, and while we ate, Lisa, Jack, and I told each other the weird jet-lagged dreams we'd had.

By seven o'clock we'd delve into language drills, cultural instruction, methods for teaching English, strategies for sharing and discipleship. We took turns practicing our teaching in front of the group. I caught Jack's eye when another teacher gave a pronunciation lesson in a rich Texas accent. Overwhelmed and exhausted, we began giggling at the thought of our Asian students speaking English with a southern drawl, and we couldn't stop.

Another day our language coach dropped us off in the open-air market with billfolds full of strange new currency. Practicing words we'd just learned, we stepped from one stall to the next on dusty dirt paths. Freshly slaughtered pigs and chickens hung under tent ceilings. I picked up a package of instant noodles and tentatively asked, "How much is this?" I marveled when I managed to understand the answer.

Along with language for bargaining, we were trained to respond to the most common questions natives would ask us: How old are you? Where are you from? Are you married? Do you want a native husband? (Don't tell Grandma.)

Near the end of training we went to the touristy part of town for a dinner that cost more than our usual fifty-cent meals. I was headachy and withdrawn as I watched the people in the restaurant, wondering if it was okay for us to spend so much on a meal—five or six dollars—when we were supposed to be *ems*. We never referred to ourselves as missionaries, but sometimes used the abbreviation "M."

By the front window I saw a couple of backpackers. She wore braids and a kerchief, while his hair was in almost-dreadlocks. Over a couple of drinks, they sat silently. He wrote a card and she studied a guidebook; after a few minutes they switched, and she read and approved his letter to be sent home.

Watching them filled me with a weird envy. What was I doing, teaching English? I wanted the backpackers' freedom—all my possessions on my back, no plans, no expectations or requirements, just going or staying and reading and writing and watching. I wanted to float across a continent again, as I'd done in college, when I spent a summer traveling through Europe: sleeping on thin bunk beds on rocking trains, waking as German officials shouted, "Schnell! Schnell!" and opening the train windows to smell the dewy green smells of a new country, clutching steaming paper cups of coffee and hard rolls. Showering inconsistently, hiking alone on paths marked "*Wanderweg*," meeting other like-minded travelers in small coastal towns, watching the sun set from a hostel balcony. I didn't want to have to think about how my habits of living looked to the people around me, whether or not it was okay to spend five dollars on a meal when my future students might be able to eat for a week on that much money.

At times our in-country training did have some of that backpacker feel, though; after five days in the capital we took a bus into the mountains, a remote countryside spot inhabited by a minority group of Thai descent.

"This doesn't look good," Lisa remarked as our van began to snake up into the hills.

"Do you get carsick?" I asked. She shook her head. "We'll get there," I assured her optimistically.

Navy storm clouds sped across the sky, and we fishtailed on the rough dirt roads. The rain slowed us, made the ruts on the narrow roads deeper and our bounces higher.

Jack strummed awkwardly on his guitar in the back of the bus to the fawning adoration of several female teachers. I turned my back to them, focusing instead on my novel, avoiding the view out the window of the steep drop below us.

In the village we stayed in a house on stilts, a kind of tree house that reminded me of the Swiss Family Robinson. The structure had one open room, with thin wooden floors and woven mats on which we ate and slept, played cards and told stories. The walls boasted posters of Asian pop stars, curling with age at the edges, outdated calendars with painted scenery, straggly tinsel, and a torn world map on which familiar places bore exotic names.

When the rain stopped, we walked outside, through rice paddies and running water, over orange dirt and green hills, among bamboo houses with straw-thatched roofs. The mist that came in with the rain draped itself across the hills and into the mountains, making the unworldly place even more magical.

Down the road we met little girls with deep eyes and warm smiles, selling friendship bracelets they'd made. From their mothers I bought brightly colored fabric wall hangings. Later, a group of us borrowed bicycles to explore further. Some tired and turned back, but Jack and I continued, talking about Flannery O'Connor, poetry, obscure bands, our sisters. I felt the wind in my hair and realized I was smiling.

• • •

"I'm afraid your teaching visas still haven't come in," Camille told us a few days later. Lisa and I were in the living room of Camille's house in the capital, waiting for our laundry to finish in the dryer. Most of the teachers would leave the next morning, dispersing throughout the country to begin work at their various universities. But because our university had been late with our initial paperwork, Lisa and I had entered the country on tourist visas, which were set to expire.

"So what will we do?" Lisa asked.

"We're going to get you on a flight to Bangkok this week," Camille answered. "When your teaching visas are ready, we'll have them sent to embassy there, and then you can reenter the country. This kind of stuff just happens sometimes." She smiled apologetically.

Secretly, I was thrilled. Another country for my passport, more backpacking and freedom.

A few days later, Lisa and I joined Australian backpackers, French tourists, and a family of suntanned Italians on a plane to Bangkok, where we would wait and pray for visas.

We stayed at a Baptist guesthouse at the end of a long, dirt road. On the river behind us, the city bus-on-boat began running at six in the morning,

which was still an hour and a half after the rooster started crowing. We were out the door early every day, buying milky sweet coffee in plastic bags, hot corn waffles, and fried bananas from street vendors. Lisa made a pleasant travel partner, easygoing and polite. She was about ten years older than I was, and took the lead in navigation as we explored the city. We didn't have much in common, but she told me about Canadian hockey teams and her niece and nephew, and I told her about Charley.

"You're still with him?" she asked, when I said that though Charley and I had broken up the previous year, we were still sort of in a relationship.

"Yeah." I tried to explain. "See, while we were broken up last year, we both decided independently to move to Asia and he seemed to have changed, to have grown more mature, so . . . I don't know, it seemed like a sign. I guess we're back together."

"Hmm," Lisa said. "I thought maybe you and Jack . . ."

"No, I mean . . ." I blushed. "Yeah, I like him, but. Anyway. We're not supposed to date this year." That was our organization's policy for first-year teachers, but since Charley and I had been together before moving to Asia, we were kind of an exception.

"What about you?" I asked, glad to change the subject. "Is there anyone you're interested in?"

When our girl talk wound down, we prayed together about our visas and our future students. As the days in Bangkok lengthened and our prayers increased, my wanderlust started to fade. And I even began to doubt its value. What if my hunger for adventure, new sights, independence, and freedom was just as dangerous, in its own way, as the lust for comfort could be? Was there something unhealthy about the kind of wandering I craved? Was it symptomatic of a larger problem, of an inability to commit to places or to people? Why was I so afraid of a mortgage and a husband, of a career and a hometown, of settling down?

I started to develop a longing to unpack my backpack, to settle into our new home and meet our students.

3

· · · · ·

Expats Will Change
the World

Areas where Protestant missionaries had a significant presence in the past are on average more economically developed today, with comparatively better health, lower infant mortality, lower corruption, greater literacy, higher educational attainment (especially for women), and more robust membership in nongovernmental associations.

Robert Woodberry, in *American Political Science Review* (2012)

Finally our visas were in, and we left the bejeweled golden temples of the land of smiles, the land of Pizza Huts and night markets and cooking classes that teach white people how to shake a wok over a fire. We flew back to the capital of our host country, our bags weighed down with new purchases from Thailand: striped coffee mugs, jars of peanut butter, an acoustic guitar. A school van met us, taking us through long stretches of quiet rice fields toward our new home. The heartland of this country, like the heartland of America, is farmland, and our students would be mostly the children of farmers, hoping to support their financially struggling families with stable English teacher salaries.

Experienced teachers had warned us not to expect much from our university-provided accommodations. We'd heard stories of cockroach infestations, dead rats, inches of grime. Lisa and I arrived on campus on a Saturday, in the hottest part of the day, mid-afternoon. School officials welcomed us awkwardly with the little English they knew, and called in male students to carry our luggage up the five flights to our rooms.

We paused, sweating and out of breath, halfway up the 101 stairs to the fifth floor. Looking off the balcony, we could see all of campus: two long, low rows of classrooms, an auditorium, some scattered small buildings, and another five story dormitory opposite us. The dusty roads were lined with small trees, and for the moment, campus was quiet. Although classes met six days a week, including Saturdays, everything shut down for a couple hours after lunch for the campus-wide siesta.

At the top of the smooth, yellow cement stairway, we found our rooms. Three rooms, just alike—the first for me, the second for Lisa, and the third to be our kitchen/office. My room was simple, like a nice dorm room, outfitted with a desk, a double bed, a plywood dresser, and a mini-fridge. Off the back, a toilet, shower, and sink. A bit dusty and gecko-haunted, but perfectly livable.

This would be home base for changing the world, even if all that meant was that we helped a few teenagers learn English so they could have stable jobs in the future.

We set to cleaning and unpacking. On the following day, we were given our teaching schedules; the day after that, we began teaching. With only two full days in our new home, barely time to unpack and figure out where to obtain food, we were flung into work, writing our own curricula, teaching groups of thirty to thirty-five undergraduates how to speak, write, read, and listen to English.

On the first day of class I woke at 5:30, when it was still dark and quiet outside, still feeling like the middle of the night. I flipped on my overhead lights and the electric water heater, then flopped back into bed until the water boiled, praying in disconnected phrases while I tried to wake up. By 6:00 music and announcements in a language I couldn't understand were blaring over the campus loudspeakers, and I could hear students in the dorms across from my building calling to each other.

After a rushed half-cup of Nescafé 3 in 1 (an instant coffee with milk and sugar), I stepped into clothes and packed my satchel. At 6:15, the sun was already bright and hot, and the campus active and loud. I crossed a couple of streets and passed dozens of students wearing their traditional

dress, required every Monday. I ascended 72 steps to my classroom, and set up for the students.

The classroom had the same floor tile pattern as my apartment, maroon and gold flowers swirling in squares. Students would sit three to a desk, on wooden benches, facing the long, green chalkboards in the front of the room. Air conditioning was only a dream in these buildings, but we occasionally got a breeze through the barred windows or the open door. When class began at 6:30, sweat was already trickling down the small of my back.

I would teach Speaking and Listening to third-year students. The room went silent when I entered, but whispers and giggles erupted from the back corners as I unpacked my satchel and wrote my name on the blackboard. After introducing myself, I gave the students an assignment: "Turn to the person next to you. Tell her about the best teacher you ever had, and what made that teacher so good."

Twenty-eight girls and five boys turned to each other, and the room filled with voices. I paced up and down the aisles between desks, listening in. They blushed and paused when I came close, then kept talking, wide-eyed and gesturing with busy hands.

At this school undergrads were formed into cohorts by year and major—these groups would take all their classes together for four years. My third-years were comfortable with each other and had the benefit of a year with a foreign English teacher before I showed up, so they weren't confused by my strange ways—requiring them to do their own homework instead of copying others, for example, or asking them to be silent rather than chattering while I taught, or basing their grades on weekly assignments rather than on one test at the end of the semester.

Teaching—a career I had never once considered while studying English literature in college—turned out to be a delight. I found that I adored poring over books in our small teaching library, exploring lesson plans online (when our dial-up internet connection allowed), and using those resources to come up with my own curriculum. But the icing on the cake was the students, who were up for anything from mock debates to acting out a simple English version of *A Midsummer Night's Dream*, which they did with costumes of their own design, melodramatic swords, and near kisses.

It took me about a month of teaching before I realized I wasn't living like a backpacker anymore. I'd moved my clothes from the backpack to the dresser, placed pictures on my desk, and bought a new scarlet bedspread. I had become that close cousin of the backpacker, the expat, making my life in a foreign place as one perpetually outside the local culture. As much as Lisa

and I tried to live like locals—shopping in the open air market, eating street food at sidewalk cafés, slurping noodles for breakfast, buying rice-flavored ice cream bars from small men pushing freezers on wheels—our skin tone made blending in impossible. Going to the market was exhausting when all the sellers wanted to touch us, hardly believing we could be real.

Sometimes we'd ride motorbike taxis over to the small, air-conditioned grocery store on the other side of town, where only foreigners and the very rich shopped, just for a break from being the center of attention. It remained impossible to find bacon or shrink-wrapped meat of any kind, but we took what we could get. Lisa bought breakfast cereal and non-refrigerated, "shelf-stable" milk (there was no fresh milk in town), and I bought a block of cheese from Australia. We relaxed at the cash register, paying the sticker price for the food. That allowed us to avoid the mental stress of bargaining—should I try to pay the same amount as the locals? Should I be willing to pay a higher "foreigner" price since I do, after all, have more resources? Which will make me most acceptable to the locals?

We might have lived more like expats if we had the choice, but there was hardly any expat community in this war-torn province—no way to indulge our longing for our home culture in foreign restaurants, no English bookstores, no Dunkin' Donuts or KFC like we'd found in Bangkok. When we tired of the constant attention our skin color earned us, or at night when it wasn't totally safe for us to go out alone, we would retreat to our apartments, eating scrambled eggs and fried potatoes and watching *The West Wing* on DVD.

Lisa and I had been told there were no other Americans in our poor farming town, but there were just a few other expats. One night we met them for dinner at the Lotus Restaurant, on the lake at the edge of town. We were there to be polite, I think, more than to make friends. I went out of curiosity, too. I knew why I'd moved to this country, but why had they?

In the large, empty room, we gathered around three tables loosely pushed together. We were sweating despite the night breeze through the open windows. Outside the sky was already black, and the hotel lights and street lights were reflecting on the surface of the lake.

The Frenchwoman wanted a revolution. "I do not say that we can change anything," she said dramatically, her voice tinged with a French accent. She was dark-skinned, short and plump, with large lips and black eyes. "But we cannot just sit by and say nothing when injustice is occurring!" Violette, in her fifties and luxuriously dogmatic, had just told a story about her top student, who had been told she needed to pay a bribe to begin work on her master's degree; after she paid the bribe, she was still denied admission.

Ann, a red-headed Canadian in her twenties, backed Violette. Her words were just barely slurred by her second light beer. "Yeah, I mean, I'm not saying we are going to start a revolution among the people or anything," she began. "God, that's not what we're here for. I'm not even saying in twenty years anything will have changed. But we have to start by at least talking about it. Acknowledging that corruption exists."

Violette taught French at the university where Lisa and I worked, and Ann was a Fulbright Scholar. The others at the table, all men, were in town for a short time to provide farming and irrigation systems training.

The Canadian next to Violette, a man with immense black eyebrows, finally got his chance to jump in. "But the problem is *systemic*," he argued. "You're never going to change anything from the bottom up in a corrupt system. You've got to change the whole system. You've got to begin at the top." His father was a politician in Canada and Ann told me later that she thought he was full of himself, that he talked to the rest of us as if we were children.

Violette unconsciously drew her silk scarf from around her neck to around her shoulders, alternately tugging each end. "Yes, but why will the politicians change anything? They do not need to. They already live in the four-story houses and drive the expensive cars. The *système* works for them."

Violette and the Canadian Eyebrows went at it for another six rounds, each making points that rarely had any real reference to each other. The waif-skinny sunburned German man nodded off at the table, and the Finnish man seemed exuberant just to be part of an English conversation.

As the youngest in the group, by quite a bit, I sat listening, admiring Violette's passion, aware of my own uncertainty. Lisa didn't say much either. The discussion introduced us to a common expat dilemma: How could we respect another culture while also desiring to rid it of injustice? I didn't have any answers. I hadn't come to this place thinking of Systems or Injustice: I had come thinking only of individuals and Jesus. But I'd started to see that the needs of the people I came to serve might be more complex than I had realized—and to wonder if my role as a teacher made me complicit in the university system's corruption.

I wondered if our expat dinner, this odd grouping on a lonely lake, this international discussion broken every half hour by the sound of a train rushing by, meant anything. We were the few foreigners living in the Middle of Nowhere, Asia, the World. Though we were in what was known as the most revolutionary province in our country, it seemed to hold little promise for changing the world anytime soon.

Despite our talk, *we* seemed to hold little promise for changing the world anytime soon either.

By the fourth round of beers—theirs, not mine, since Lisa and I were observing our organization's policy against drinking—the political clash of ideas really began. I felt I was being drawn into the scene of a Hemingway novel, with our city an unfortunate 2003 replacement for Paris, the expats trying to make sense of life in the corner of a dark café. There's a similar kind of despair and loneliness and passion in the air, though little of the glamour of the French capital.

We were the strangers in town, I thought to myself as we dispersed on bicycles, in a car, on a motorbike. We were the ones who, for many unknown reasons, had given up life in western countries to live in this small rural town—but did we even know enough of this culture to begin to think of changing it? I was sure, as I pedaled away, that the top-down, change-the-system approach espoused by the Canadian had merit, as did the idealistic, fight-oppression-and-injustice (*liberté, egalité, fraternité*) approach championed by the French woman. But I wondered about our motivations. I had gone to this place wanting to do something grand too, but now I wondered if I understood what that meant. Have we even learned enough about this country to earn the right to want to change things? Should I focus solely on teaching English, evangelism, and discipleship, or could I work for systemic justice as well?

We were all full of ourselves at dinner, bandying about our theories as if we had within ourselves the power to do great things. Maybe we did have an influence to wield within the university, a privilege we could leverage on behalf of our poor students. We should do that, and we should work to make unjust systems just. Yet we were still foreigners, with no guarantee that we could affect this culture from our outsiders' position. And even if we could make changes, wouldn't some of the corruption remain?

After all, corruption is not just bound to a system; it is intrinsic to the human heart. The best hope for change comes from people who understand both kinds of corruption—and who recognize the corruption in our own prideful hearts as well.

4

· · · · ·

Do Not Easily Leave

It is a prolonged system of picnicking, excellent for the health, and agreeable to those who are not over-fastidious about trifles, and who delight in being in the open air.

David Livingstone, describing arduous travel
in the uncharted interior of Africa

Of course it costs life. It is not an expedition of ease nor a picnic excursion to which we are called. It is going to cost many a life, and not lives only, but prayers and tears and blood.

Samuel Zwemer, the "Apostle to Islam"

On my twenty-first birthday, I was alone in France. Well, not entirely alone: I was staying at Taizé, an ecumenical monastic community, along with hundreds of other pilgrims. But none of them knew it was my birthday, of course. Near five o'clock, I made my way to the counter of the open-air café that sold snacks every afternoon. I ordered a single plastic cup of red wine and toasted myself, twenty-one, alone and free.

Then David, a new friend I'd made at Taizé, joined me. "Hey," he said, plopping his gangly, green-eyed, curly-haired self on the bench next to me. I liked him. "How was your day?" he asked. "You didn't come to the Bible study."

Every day at Taizé began with communal prayer in the candlelit chapel. Swaths of reddish orange fabric hung from ceiling to floor, like tongues of fire descending, and I meditated, open-eyed, as I learned the chants we'd sing in Latin, French, Spanish, English, and Italian.

After morning prayer, each of us received a baguette with butter, a cup of coffee, and a square of dark chocolate (which to this day is my ideal breakfast). Each newcomer was assigned a community responsibility, and mine was dishes: after the meal I joined a group of teenage Irish boys in the kitchen to clean up. Later we had midday prayer, lunch, optional workshops and group Bible studies led by monks, time for silence and contemplation, supper, and evening prayer. I'd skipped the optional Bible study that day.

"I spent the afternoon by the lake, in silence," I told David. "Well, I wanted it to be silence—there were some construction trucks on the other side of the lake. Kind of drove me crazy." I paused, wanting to keep talking with him. "So, how did you find out about Taizé?" I asked.

"The University of Virginia gave me a fellowship to study the spirituality of monastic communities in Europe," he said, "So I've been traveling around. What about you?"

I felt a little out of my league. "I just finished a semester in Italy," I said. "When classes ended, I backpacked with some friends for a while. They're all stateside now, so I'm here by myself for a week before I head home."

Silence drew out awkwardly. I watched people ordering snacks at the counter, and listened to the birds singing around us. "I love backpacking," I said finally. "And I love being here—it's so different from the kind of spirituality I grew up with. But I can't imagine making a monastic kind of commitment—agreeing to stay in one place forever."

I wondered if David was Catholic. If he wanted to be a monk.

"Do you know how Taizé started?" he asked. I shook my head.

"Brother Roger started Taizé in 1940, while France was in the middle of World War II," David said. "He came from Switzerland. His idea was to make a place where people who were wounded or hopeless could find work and peace. Soon men came from around the world to join. It's one of the only monastic communities that has monks who are Catholic, Protestant, and Orthodox."

"He was kind of like a missionary," I mused. The not-too-distant bells rang, calling us to prayer.

These men left their homes to join Taizé—but then they stayed. The power of their venture was only realized through a commitment to planting roots.

That night I dug out a sheaf of papers I'd been carrying around Europe with me—a bunch of sermons that preached verse by verse through Hebrews 11.

I thought that was the perfect chapter to study while backpacking, because it commended heroes of faith who "acknowledged that they were strangers and exiles on the earth," who were "seeking a homeland"—and not the one they'd left.

That was my favorite metaphor for the Christian life, because I never really felt at home where I was, either. If I were a "sojourner," then I could be free to float along, unconcerned about fitting in, without becoming overly invested, safe from the complications of relationships. I always got twitchy when I stayed still too long: I took weekend road trips, bought last minute plane tickets. I changed the subject any time Charley tried to get serious about settling down.

David and I wandered down to the chapel. I thought about asking him for his e-mail address, or asking him to send me a copy of his research paper when he finished it, but I was too scared. I never saw him again.

• • •

Sometimes I recalled my conversation with David at Taizé while I worked on grad school assignments in the evenings in Asia. For one paper, I was supposed to research a missionary or a missionary movement. I chose the desert fathers and mothers, the very first Christians who retreated from their world to find a purer spirituality. Eventually they formed communities together, communities like Taizé, committed to a place. Later, some of those communities sent missionaries out to new places.

One of the books I was reading was *The Sayings of the Desert Fathers*, translated by Benedicta Ward. It's a paperback with glowing golden icons on the cover, Jesus and a monk with long faces and halos. I was highlighting it at my desk one afternoon when I heard footsteps in the hallway outside. I opened the door.

"Come in!" Four girls from one of my classes entered shyly. Minnie was holding a tiny kitten. "Miss Amy, I think you are lonely," she began. "You said you like a cat."

"Yes, I would like a cat. You brought me a cat? This is so sweet!" I held the tiny striped animal close to my chest. It mewed fiercely, its whole body thumping with fear.

"Please, sit down and have some tea," I urged the girls.

"We can't stay," they answered.

"Oh, really?" I asked. "Well—" I paused. I didn't know enough about the culture yet to realize that the girls wouldn't accept my invitation to tea unless I repeated it several times. "What should I feed the cat?"

They looked at each other, conferring with language I couldn't comprehend.

"Maybe some fish," they said.

"Okay." This would be a challenge.

"Bye, teacher, see you tomorrow," they said, heading down the stairs.

After they left, I set the kitten on the floor. She leapt away from me, hiding herself under my bed. I couldn't reach her, and she just kept mewing. She was probably too young to leave her mother. And now I needed to figure out how to buy the right kind of fish for her. Feeling overwhelmed, I decided to wait until Lisa returned from her class. She'd help me figure it all out. In the meantime, I returned to my book.

The first and most famous of the desert fathers, St. Anthony, was once asked, "What must one do in order to please God?" His answer had three parts:

"Whoever you may be, always have God before your eyes; whatever you do, do it according to the testimony of the holy Scriptures; in whatever place you live, do not easily leave it."

As I read about these monks who stayed quietly in the same places, doing the same tasks and praying the same prayers for years and years, I began to wonder if my own definition of sojourner was missing something. Had I misunderstood this metaphor? Or worse, had I been using a false idea to excuse my own wanderlust, my desire for independence, and my fear of commitment?

When Peter wrote to the elect resident aliens scattered throughout the Roman provinces of Asia Minor, he was writing to Christians facing persecution: his description of them as sojourners and exiles, whether literal or metaphorical, was intended to help them understand how to live with patience and holiness as an oppressed minority in the empire. It was a reminder that Christians ought to live with "reverent fear" wherever we are, aware that our truest identity is as citizens of a different Kingdom.

But I'd been using the title *sojourner* to justify my rootlessness. I wasn't persecuted or oppressed. I hadn't been forced into exile. I was simply exercising my privilege and freedom to leave my home, safe with a passport to bring me back when I was ready. I was at the top, not the bottom, of the day's empire economies. To claim that metaphor for my own was to discredit the very real persecution that originally undergirded it.

Here's the thing I began to realize about my wanderlust, as I listened to the bewildered cries of my displaced kitten: I was not an exile. I was not a mythic hero out to conquer a new frontier, finding freedom in the wild blue yonder. To put it plainly, I was discovering that restlessness is not always a virtue. For anyone to have a meaningful presence in the world, at some point the desire to *go* must transform into a desire to *stay*.

So I took the small steps that were the only things I knew to do to practice staying put. I named my kitten Éponine, after a tragic Victor Hugo character who lived on her own, and I figured out how to find food for her. I met the Thai exchange students who lived on the floor beneath me. I had a regular photocopy shop, where the owners made fun of me for using the wrong personal pronouns to address them, and a bakery I visited every day for loaves of French bread. I left my apartment door open so students would know they could come visit.

For the time being, I tried to remind myself that I wasn't there to save the world or to indulge my independent spirit. I temporarily shelved any grand ideas about fixing structural injustices and instead practiced the small, daily, rooted tasks that are, after all, also a part of doing justice and loving mercy, those simple things the monks also practiced. I made it my ambition to lead a quiet life, and to lead that quiet life *where I was*, while trying to learn from the people around me. I aimed to become a student of their language and their culture, to find out what love looked like to them.

I was no longer a backpacker. I wasn't an expat—at least, I was trying not to be. Instead, I was beginning to figure out what it means to be a neighbor.

Interlude

A BRIEF HISTORY
OF SHORT-TERM MISSIONS

Only fifty years ago, my stint teaching in Southeast Asia would have been considered a "short-term mission" trip. It's worth pausing here, with my perspective on my life overseas beginning to shift, to consider the genesis and development of the short-term mission.

For much of Christian history, a call to international missions had been considered lifelong; some early missionaries shipped their necessities in a coffin, assuming they wouldn't come home except to be buried. But as travel technologies improved, home furloughs became possible, then standard. Shorter terms of service became realistic options. And then very short trips— even ten to fourteen days—became common for laypeople and youth.

Short-term mission trips as we know them today began in the 1960s. The success of projects like the Peace Corps, paired with the growth of mass commercial air travel, inspired Christian organizations to experiment. Recruiting primarily college students and single twenty-somethings, organizations like YWAM (Youth With A Mission) and OM (Operation Mobilization) created cross-cultural experiences that lasted from a month to a year or two. A narrative grew up about these trips: they were ways for American young people to gain spiritual insight and grow personally while serving "the least of these." Individual churches adopted the trend and set up their own trips, too.

But established missionary boards and agencies were slower to adopt short-term missions, and when they did, the narrative was different: it was less about spiritual formation for the young people and more about helping established missionaries—even recruiting new, long-term missionaries. The

boards didn't view short-termers as missionaries, but as *potential* missionaries. The Southern Baptist "Journeyman" program, founded in 1965, for example, featured a two-year term with the goal of exposing young people "to missionary life while serving career goals of established missionaries." In the late sixties, Africa Inland Mission had short-term options of one to two years available, but promotional materials encouraged missionaries to always have long-term service as their goal.

It was not until the 1970s that high school students began to take part in short-term mission experiences. Summer youth trips gained widespread acceptance in the 1980s, and by the 1990s, they had exploded in popularity. The established missionary community, faced with the ubiquity of short-term trips, was forced to concede: finally, they too began calling them "missions trips," and referring to people who made one- or two-year commitments overseas as "missionaries."

So you might say that in the brief history of short-term mission trips, there have been two competing narratives to justify their existence: the established missionary community wanted the story to be about recruiting potential missionaries and aiding established missionaries, but local churches and new organizations wanted the story to be about the spiritual growth of those who went, along with serving the poor (not traditionally a goal of missionary work, which had primarily been about evangelism, Scripture translation, and church planting). This second narrative, for the most part, won out in the American evangelical community.

And this is why when people come back from a short-term trip, you'll hear them say things like, "They [the poor] taught me so much more than I taught them," or "They gave me so much more than I gave them." This is the narrative their preparation has primed them to use. They had been told that they were going to serve the poor and experience spiritual growth; they're simply saying that their spiritual growth seems more valuable than their service was.

And undoubtedly, in a lot of cases, that's true! Especially if the service they've gone to provide was a project their church dreamed up, rather than something the people they served had asked for.

For example, suppose a church knows of a school in a Latin American country that needs a new building. They send a team of high schoolers to do the work, a common enough type of summer trip experience. But suppose that while these students—inexperienced in the art of building, but happy to serve—are working on the construction, a man from the community walks by. He's bigger and stronger than the kids are. He's unemployed. When he looks

at them, he sees teenagers who have enough extra money to fly to his country, doing a job for free that he would have loved to have been paid even a small wage to do. Those wages would have gone to feed his family, or to enable him to buy the uniforms his children must have to attend that very school.

This building team has helped the community, yes, but probably not in the best way. They've flown in like little gods, fixed a problem, and flown out again, leaving community members feeling even more helpless than before. Those teens wore their matching T-shirts emblazoned with "Bringing God to [insert country name here]!" as if God hasn't been there all along. Maybe they have—unwittingly—*used* the poor for their own spiritual growth.

Admittedly, this is just one example from a multitude of kinds of short-term trips. There are ways we've done them well, and ways we've done them not so well. But for now, let's just talk about the language: Should we really call a trip like this, one we've just admitted does more for us than it does for the people we serve, a *missions* trip?

What if, instead, we called them "vision trips" or "learning trips"? A simple renaming might change the whole way we plan, prepare for, and experience such trips.

Imagine someone asking for financial support for a "vision trip." Instead of saying, "Please give me money so that I can take the gospel to a dark place / build a house for the homeless / run a summer camp program for kids in Haiti / assist in a temporary medical clinic in Tegucigalpa," a short-termer might say, "If you would like to invest in me, would you help me travel to a different culture so that I can expand my view of who God is and how he works by learning about him in a foreign land?"

In preparing short-termers for their trips, we'd treat them like children about to visit an art museum. With training and education, children can progress from seeing everything but understanding almost nothing to really grasping what they do see. We can prepare them to learn from the museum guide. We can give them historical, social, and artistic language to use in describing their experience. Likewise, it would make sense for people preparing for a "vision trip" to learn about the history, language, economic structures, and ethnic groups of the community they're about to visit so that when they arrive, they'll be better able to understand what they see.

When they went, short-termers would be ready to listen to locals, to learn from them. And they'd be able to integrate all the parts of their trip. Instead of dividing them into "ministry" and "tourism," every aspect of the experience—even visits to famous sites, shopping in the markets, and attending a local church—would be a part of a cohesive learning experience.

Dr. David Zac Niringiye was assistant bishop of the Kampala diocese of the Anglican Church in Uganda. When asked if short-term mission trips could serve African Christians well, he suggested that short-term trips ought to be oriented around listening. What if, he said, instead of going with a "mission" in mind, Americans just brought greetings from one church to another, and opened up a conversation, a relationship?

"Short-term mission" has been part of our lexicon for less than fifty years, and it's the wrong name. Let's change the term, and let that simple change lead us to a more reciprocal, authentic, relational model, one oriented around listening. Let's be sure we in the West are aware of our cultural power, we use our social capital to help, and we learn about structural injustices instead of just witnessing poverty. Let's make our trips about cross-cultural communication and relationship, and let's line them up with the mission of God, which is long-term by definition: the restoration of relationships, the reconciliation of all things to himself.

Of course, "vision trip" might not be the right name, either. My own trip to Southeast Asia would enlighten me, yes—but then it would leave me in the dark for a long time before my vision cleared again.

5

. . . . .

The Strictest American

Let us adopt their costume, acquire their language, study to imitate their habits, and approximate to their diet as far as health and constitution will allow.

Hudson Taylor, speaking of the Chinese

One Saturday, a few weeks into the semester, Tina called us around eight in the morning. "Are you awake yet?" she asked Lisa, knowing her well enough by now to realize she's struggling to get out of bed. I love the early morning, but Lisa's a night owl. "When are we going to eat yogurt again?" Tina asked.

Soon she was at the door. Lisa and I had scrambled into clothes, and we went just outside the campus walls, around the corner to our favorite café. It's like a garage, a cement-floored room open to the street. We sat on child-sized blue plastic stools around a child-sized red plastic table, the customary seating at most street cafés in our city. Tina opened the small chest freezer just inside the café and brought us three glasses of plain yogurt. She picked metal spoons from the cutlery holder on our table, expertly rubbing them with thin paper napkins before handing them to us. "Enjoy," she said, her playful eyes sparkling, and we did.

Tina was a third year student, a class monitor and the daughter of the vice president of the university, which meant she was with us at least partly out

of a sense of duty. We were teachers, and because of that it was her cultural responsibility to show us honor and respect. We were also foreigners, which meant it is her cultural responsibility to show us hospitality—and to keep an eye on us.

Over cold, creamy bites of yogurt, we asked Tina questions. She preferred not to discuss her older, pock-faced, parent-approved boyfriend, but she admitted to us that her dream was to someday be headmistress of a university. The fact that we couldn't think of *any* university with a female head in this country only made her more serious about the goal.

Tina was just a year or two younger than I was, and I felt a natural affinity with her: she was smart, ambitious, wary of romance, and extremely competent. She teased me about my lack of skill with chopsticks. "You eat like a baby," she said, smirking.

"Actually, we haven't been eating much at all," interjected Lisa. "We need to go to the market."

"Yes, I will take you," Tina said. She paid for our yogurt, and when we protested, told us, "I invited, so it's my treat. Next time, though, you must invite me." This is what made Tina one of our most valuable friends: in a country where much is silently implied and understood, she was willing to be blunt. She served as our cultural informant, somehow aware of exactly which things ignorant westerners needed to have explained, like this—whoever invites pays, and reciprocity is the foundation for relationship. There are no split tickets here.

"What do you need to buy?" Tina asked as we headed toward the collection of blue tarp tents that made up our local street market. We'd learned enough language to buy some things. I could ask how much something cost, or say that I wanted six eggs. I could pick out potatoes, loaves of French bread, bananas, and packages of instant noodles.

"We need help buying chicken," I admitted. "Can you ask them to cut just the breast meat off the bone for us?" Once I explained what I meant by "chicken breast" (body language helped), Tina raised an eyebrow skeptically, but turned to a meat seller and began a long conversation. We couldn't really follow it, except to see that the seller almost refused to sell the breasts alone, and that after she finally agreed, Tina had to argue for a price somewhat lower than a "charge foreigners twice as much" amount. "Do you want the bones, too?" Tina asked. When Lisa and I declined, it was clear both Tina and the seller thought we were wasteful.

"There." She handed us the bag. "If you come back to this seller, she'll know to cut the breasts off for you," she informed us. "What else?" It took a

while to communicate to Tina that I wanted sugar and flour—not flowers, not rice flour, but wheat flour—but she took us to a stall with barrels full of white powders, and helped us buy a pound of each.

We continued down the dirt path, lined on each side with wizened nut-brown women, sitting on their heels next to woven baskets full of green vegetables I'd never seen before or enormous tin bowls filled with water and shrimp and squid motored in from the coast, fifteen kilometers (a little over nine miles) away. A bony woman with stained lips expertly spit betel juice from the corner of her mouth, then grabbed my leg, asking a question I couldn't understand. Tina answered her scornfully, then told me, "She asked if you were native."

"What?" I was confused. How could she even think I might be native? This country was a monoculture: everyone around me was slender, with straight, black hair and dark eyes. I'm blond and blue-eyed.

"She thinks you're too skinny to be American," Tina explained. "In fact, she wouldn't believe me. She argued that you must be Thai." I asked Tina if she was teasing me again.

"No," Tina said. "We all wondered if you were really American when you first got here. Any Americans we'd seen before were big and tall, but you weren't." Finally convinced that I was, in fact, American, Tina told me that they had decided that I must be the strictest American. I didn't see how that followed, so she explained: "You don't dress like Britney Spears at all!"

Finally we exited the market. Tina didn't give a second glance to the legless beggar who sat at the entrance, though I always wondered who did help him, what my role ought to be, or if my home country had anything to do with his long-ago injury.

There was little sense of individual responsibility to the poor or injured in this nation. Once, in the capital city, I witnessed a motorbike accident—two bikes went down, their drivers certainly injured. The streets were constantly clogged with motorbikes and only a few cars, and none of the drivers gave any thought to traffic rules. Nor did they care about the crash victims. No one stopped or rushed over to help. The other motorbike drivers simply swerved around them and kept on.

After an accident in America, witnesses might feel compelled to stop—to assist the injured, to call 911, to report details to the police. In this country, though, no one feels that compunction unless they know the people in the accident—and not just know them, but consider them part of their in-group. In this collectivist culture, you owed nothing to strangers; but you owed everything to your in-group.

I was confused by what this might mean for me. It was clear what it meant to my students. The importance of knowing their place within the group shaped their lives. Their parents made their decisions with them, sometimes even finding their dates for them. The family, not the individual, was the first and most important unit of survival. The students' networks of friends were tight and intense. Many of my students told me about their primary anxiety as they entered university: would they find people to "share life's happiness and sadness with," they wondered? A group of friends in one of my classes had even nicknamed themselves "the family," giving each other roles within the group: father, mother, grandfather, little sister.

After family and close friends, the university cohort became a third identifying group. No one made friends outside their class. Within the cohort, the monitor led the group in making sure that every member succeeded in school. When homework was assigned, the monitor would ask one smart student to complete it so everyone else could copy the work. The success of the group meant more than recognition for the individual.

I was beginning to grasp the implications of this, the way it makes relationships more important than tasks or efficiency. It explained why, when I walked through town in the afternoons, I saw a line of men sitting on their heels, looking out toward the sea. They weren't doing anything; they were just being together. It explained why, if I ran into a student on campus on her way to rehearsal, she joined me for coffee first; our relationship was more important than punctuality. And the importance of in-group relationship even affected the understanding of what was ethical in their country. Tina told me that she once got a traffic ticket from a police officer. She paid it, but when she went home and told her family, her brother—also a policeman—got angry with her. "Why didn't you tell him you are my sister?" he demanded. "Then you wouldn't have had to pay it." In this country, the laws existed only for people you didn't know.

The tightness of relationships meant that people were often able to communicate much with only a glance or a word. They were so intimate that they didn't need to be direct. I started to recognize this, to figure out that when Tina said, "It's so hot today," what she meant is that she needed a drink or wanted me to invite her out for ice cream. When I answered her correctly, she would smile slyly and say, "I think you understand me."

But figuring out these cultural differences didn't make them easy to adjust to. I didn't want to make small talk and drink tea at the post office every time I went in—I just wanted to buy a stamp! I didn't think it was okay for one student to do homework for the whole class to copy, and I didn't think

it was acceptable to be late to meetings or rehearsals because you ran into a friend on the way! In-groups looked a lot like favoritism to me.

Yet I attempted to suspend judgment, to live in a kind of liminal state where I observed and learned rather than criticizing my host culture. Becoming all things to all people, so that by all possible means I might win some, as the apostle Paul wrote in 1 Corinthians 9, suggested that everything about my identity was on the chopping block, even my sense of right and wrong. It became an exercise in humility.

What proved most difficult for me, though, was not suspending judgment but figuring out my place in this complex web of in-groups. I wondered how closely the students were watching me to see who I spent my time with. Did I have to "belong" to a group, too, or was I, as a foreigner and a teacher, free to make close friends within several different groups? It may seem like a silly question to Americans, but in that country it mattered intensely. Unsure of what it meant for me, I decided simply to spend time with anyone who was interested, and to try to reciprocate invitations. I also made sure to do favors for important people, like the dean and other faculty members, so they would feel that I was becoming part of their in-groups. I hoped that spending time with some students more than others would not cause problems for me or anyone else.

And then one day there knocked on my door a student who was different from every other student I'd met.

6

. . . . .

Locusts and Miracles

God used my love for English to draw me to himself.

Christiana Tsai, Chinese convert

It was a warm afternoon in mid-October, and the knock was hesitant, so quiet I wasn't sure anyone was there. I opened the door to find a freshman, bearing longan fruit and a smile. Unlike most of my students, she wore neither the long traditional dress nor the standard college student outfit of fitted jeans and blouse with pointy-toed sandals. She wore all black: black pants, a long-sleeved black button-down, black shoes, and a black baseball cap turned backwards. Her teeth were crooked and her eyes, piercing. I welcomed Veronica in.

I'd recently taken on an extra class, teaching writing to freshman. Their teacher, pregnant at the time, had fallen and been put on bedrest, so the class was reassigned to me. It was a B-level class of freshmen, which meant that all the students in it had failed the university entrance exam on their first attempt. Some of them had waited a year to retake the test and gain admittance to the university; others had gotten in because their parents had paid an extra fee. Veronica was in this class, but she was older than most of her classmates.

"I failed the test two times," she admitted to me as we sat down for tea. "I wanted to study literature, but had to study English instead." When she rolled up her sleeves to peel the longan fruit, I could see the signs of despair:

her failure to be the daughter her parents hoped for lined the underside of her forearms with faint pink scars.

We chatted about our families. Veronica asked me what kind of music I liked. I hadn't figured out how to answer this question yet, since most of my students had never heard of the bands I listened to. Most of them loved older American music—the Carpenters, or Michael Jackson. Veronica was obsessed with American boy bands.

She sat politely on the woven mat on my tile floor, deftly skinning the grape-sized longan, revealing the tender, pearly fruit within.

"Are you a Christian?" she asked. "Brian in the Backstreet Boys is a Christian."

I didn't recognize it as the miracle of divinely orchestrated events that it was, not at first. The way all those details fit together: that she, who had nearly the best English in her class, had somehow failed the entrance exam two years in a row, only to switch majors so she could finally be admitted this year as a freshman. That her class wasn't originally assigned to me, but that the pregnant teacher fell and had to be put on bed rest, so I took over the class. When Veronica came to visit me that first time and asked about Jesus and the Backstreet Boys, I doubted her interest could possibly be serious. I wondered if I should dismiss her questions as easily as a pop song, silly and inconsequential.

In truth, it seemed like just one of many interesting conversations I'd had with students, who were fast becoming my friends. While smart, sarcastic Tina had shown no interest in talking about God, others had. Darcy and Anne, inseparable third-year students who'd agreed to tutor me in their language, would come up to my apartment with lists of words for me to learn, but we'd end up playing guitar and talking about boys. One night they took me to a city celebration at the center of town, to a park with a huge statue of the father of their country. We admired the statue, the fountain, and the lights at dusk, and bought yellow sticky rice ice cream from a vendor pushing a small freezer on wheels. We walked hand in hand up the hill, pausing when the girls in their high heels were out of breath. Darcy teased us: "I think there is a handsome man waiting at the top." She smiled impishly, trying to convince us to keep going. "Yes, maybe three handsome men," Anne replied, tucking her long black hair behind her ears and pushing her glasses up on her nose. They giggled and wondered if we should pretend to fall in the fountain, hoping one of the handsome men might feel compelled to rescue us.

Later, more seriously, Anne asked me to pray that she would find true love. I told her that she could ask God for that herself. "I can't," she said, "I don't know God." I offered to pray that she would know God, and she accepted my offer.

As much as I enjoyed my new friends, I didn't identify with their romantic visions. I'd never been one of those girls who dreamed of her wedding day, who wrote letters to her future husband or got crazy crushes on pop stars. I'd always been much more conflicted about marriage, about whether I wanted it or not. I approached it logically rather than emotionally, making a point to remain in control of my feelings.

Being overseas didn't make it simpler. Charley and I e-mailed nearly every day, comparing our experiences teaching in different countries, talking about students and theology and teammates and our relationship. I was always confused—I desperately missed him, I missed being known and truly seen. My students struggled to understand me and my foreign ways: I wanted to be around someone who saw me, and no one knew me better than Charley. But I still found him exasperating and immature. I loved him, but I didn't trust him. I was constantly wondering if I loved him enough to make it work, constantly wondering who I was going to be: a devoted missionary forever, a standard-issue wife and mom, or something else entirely. A PhD candidate, a novelist, a nomad.

At the end of my second month teaching, I was a bundle of contradictions. I adored my life. I adored my quiet mornings with coffee and my laptop, and the evenings alone teaching myself to play melancholy folk songs on the guitar. I adored my classes—my hilarious and outgoing third-year students, my dreamy and big-eyed first-year students. I adored teaching, and reading the essays students turned in, papers that started with lines like "When I see him, I am lovesick," or "This life is not easy for anyone," or "When I was a child, I asked my mother why I could not fly." I adored riding on the back of Darcy's motorbike, and learning how to cook with rice paper, and drinking the thick, sweet iced coffee sold on the side of the road.

But in the course of a single week I could move from joyful contentment to barren despair. I was lonely, wishing that my family and friends back home would at least e-mail me back. Their lives seemed to be moving along without me. Disconnected from so many of the people and things I'd once used to identify myself, what was left? Who was I?

It had been months since I'd attended a church or even been with a large group of Christians. I felt my spiritual wells being sucked dry. I felt barren. For one of my online grad classes, I was reading through the book of Acts. Peter's speech in chapter two quotes from the prophet Joel, his promise that in the last days God would pour out his Spirit on all flesh, that sons and daughters would prophesy.

Curious about that promise, I followed those verses back to their source, reading Joel's prophecy in full. I was struck by how the description of the

Israelites sounded like me, with all my gladness "dried up," with nothing left to offer to God. The nation of Israel had been hit by drought and a plague of locusts—a devastating plague far worse than any they had ever experienced. Their land was barren, and they had nothing to offer to God—no grain or wine to bring as temple sacrifices.

I felt dried up, too. I wanted to follow Joel's exhortation, to rend my heart and not my garments, hoping that God would "turn and have pity and leave behind a blessing." I knew what I wanted that blessing to be: success, prestige, emotional stability, clear direction for the future, easy relationships. Would God turn to me in my emptiness and offer me those things?

But that's not what Joel suggested. No, the blessing God might bestow on repentant hearts was this: grain and drink offerings for the Lord. The blessing God would give was restoration of what had been lost *so that* his people could praise him again.

I needed my desires to be transformed, so that I would grow to want more than anything else the ability to praise God.

Later in the book, God tells the Israelites that he will repay them for the years the locusts have eaten. I was bowled over by the beauty of that promise, its evocative image: that even when my sin leads to dryness and discipline, God will restore what I have lost. But I felt shaken and unsettled by it, too. The *years* the locusts have eaten. Would I lose whole years of my life to the locusts? How long would I feel empty inside?

That's where I was—emptiness, uncertainty, confusion, and joy all mixed— when Veronica came to visit me the second time.

I'd gotten to know her a bit better through her journal writings in class, and come to realize that she was a deep thinker, a poet, and a seeker. I hadn't said anything more to her about Jesus, not yet; while I described myself as a Christian when I introduced myself on the first day of classes, I hadn't said more than that to anyone.

Veronica wanted me to know that there was a Catholic church on the edge of town. Would I visit it with her on Sunday, and then eat lunch at her home, with her family?

It was still warm that November Sunday as we motorbiked to the edge of town. I was curious—skeptical, maybe, but hopeful—about what we'd find. Why had people told me there were no local Christians if this church existed? Would the church have Bibles available in the local language?

The town was quiet on Sunday mornings; shopkeepers in pajamas swept sidewalks and opened their doors. The city streets, lined with skinny three-story French colonial buildings painted in pastel colors, smelled of urine and

smoke, but as we left town, lonely rice fields swallowed us in sweet green. Around a corner, behind a gate, we came upon the church suddenly, a stone cathedral with spires, a bit of Europe in the middle of Asia. I wondered what we'd find inside: the truth, or just bits of truth mixed with traditional religion to form something new? The Spirit, or many spirits? Freedom, or fear?

Of course, I couldn't find those answers myself. The entire service took place in a foreign language, so I relied on Veronica to interpret it for me later that afternoon. We talked about some of the scriptures that were read, and the prayers and traditions. She seemed to share my skepticism, remarking that the people she spoke with there only attended because of a superstitious belief that they needed to confess to a priest in order to be safe from evil spirits or curses. But she wanted to know more. "Can we study the Bible together?" she asked me afterward.

"Of course," I replied. "Anytime you like." Back at her house, we ate rice, stir-fried pork, whole grilled fishes, sautéed spinach with garlic, pomelo fruit—a feast—prepared by her mother, a soft, round-faced woman who held and patted my arm, looking deeply into my eyes with a questioning gaze and with something like gratitude. I smiled shyly, then realized suddenly that she thought I was saving her daughter. She wasn't oblivious to the despair that had threatened to pull Veronica under since she failed the university entrance exam two years earlier. This mother didn't care what saved her daughter; she was just thankful to see her alive again, curious and engaged and happy. Veronica's father, quiet, but observant, seemed proud to be entertaining a foreigner. Her younger brother struck me as bright-eyed and sweet. I hardly knew what to do with all the kindness they showered on me.

Still I waited. Was Veronica interested in me because I was a foreigner, or was she truly interested in knowing God? I waited for her to ask again, and she did, the very next time our class met. After the other students dissipated, she came up to my desk. "When can we study the Bible together?" she asked.

That night Veronica and her friend Sarah came to my apartment after dinner. I showed them the Bible, and we talked about what kind of book it was, where it came from, who wrote it. I gave Veronica some pages I'd printed from a college Bible study, an introduction to the Bible and the first few chapters of Luke. I asked her why she was interested in studying.

"I want to belong to something," she said, struggling to find the right English words. "Did you know Brian from the Backstreet Boys went to Cincinnati Bible College? I think if I read this book, I will be . . . complete."

Veronica and I began meeting every Sunday night, talking about a few chapters of Luke each time. She asked if she could have my copy of the Bible

in her language, and I let her take it, warning her to be careful reading it in public. Each week she showed up with pages and pages of reflections and questions written in her journal. More confident writing in English than speaking, she sometimes wrote me letters. A month after we began studying together, she wrote about the way reading the Bible had changed her.

> I ever lost faith in the life. And I didn't know what the meaning of my life was. I totally lost myself until you came and let me know about Jesus' words. . . . The moment you suggested me learning the Bible, I was so afraid, that I was not good enough to receive such a great world, but I really wanted to know it. The Bible let me understand that The Father comes to us not because we are good enough, but because we are forgiven.
>
> My English is not good, I know you sympathize and see my heart for it. May I think that you are my sister? You didn't only come as a teacher, but as a messenger. I heard the Bible say that Messengers can appear through many different forms. . . .

I couldn't quite believe what was happening. For some reason, I was shocked to see the Bible work, astounded that Veronica, who had never read the Bible before, could read it for the first time and recognize exactly the same truths I'd memorized in catechism as a little girl.

Maybe it was all true, after all. I realized suddenly that I hadn't been sure. I hadn't been sure that the truths which had surrounded me since birth would still be true on the other side of the world, in a totally foreign culture. I had kind of wondered if we had made it all up. But the prayers my supporters had prayed were being answered, within the first three months I'd spent in the city—the city that everyone had warned me was a hard, dark place. The Spirit was already at work there, just like in the stories I'd read, where missionaries arrived at isolated islands or deep interior jungles to be welcomed by natives proclaiming, "We know who you are! You are messengers of God. He told us in a dream you were coming."

And so dreams and pop music led to salvation, and the miracle began in my barrenness and disbelief. I could take no credit for the miracle—it was really proof that I'm a true daughter of the biblical Sarah, who laughed at the promise of new life. God was calling Veronica to himself, and was allowing me to watch, even to take part. The locusts disappeared before they had even had time to descend. Suddenly I found myself with an offering of praise.

7

. . . . .

Long Walks on the Beach

Sometimes [Jesus] sent his disciples out to work in dark and difficult areas. . . .
Jesus reassured them by saying: "Come apart and rest awhile."

Margaret Maund, missionary from Wales to the Congo

What are we here for, to have a good time with Christians or to save sinners?

Malla Moe, Norwegian missionary to Swaziland

In so many ways, it's impossible to connect the work I do with the historic missions movement of the nineteenth century, with the experiences of those people like Hudson Taylor and Amy Carmichael who inspired my decision to move to Asia. I did not travel for two months by boat; I flew overnight on a jet. I did not wait for weeks to receive correspondence from home; I dialed up my internet connection every morning to check for e-mail, sometimes receiving long, thoughtful, nourishing epistles from my dad. Occasionally I even paid exorbitantly to call home, to hear my sister's voice from her college in New York. When I got sick, I wasn't shipped to a warmer climate to recuperate; I bought dirt-cheap antibiotics at the drugstore down the road. And if things would have gotten worse, I had international health insurance that would airlift me out of anywhere.

I was not a brave pioneer forging trails in the wilderness; I was a member of a large, well-run organization with structures in place to train and support me. I never wondered where my next meal would come from; staff in California handled my finances, and I could use my debit card at an ATM in the capital. I benefited from the sacrifices those first missionaries made and the patterns they established, but I sometimes wondered if the kind of miracles they experienced—a donation appearing out of nowhere at just the right time for Amy Carmichael to buy land for her rescued children, or violent men made calm when Gladys Aylward singlehandedly stopped a prison riot—were even needed anymore.

Two months into the semester, when Lisa and I began to feel lonely and isolated, we simply bought train tickets to the capital for a weekend. We ate hamburgers and milkshakes at an Australian restaurant, bought DVDs of *Friends*, and stole English novels from the shelves of our country director, Camille. We spoke English at a normal speed, using our full vocabularies. For weeks we had only been speaking slowly, using simple words and lots of hand gestures to communicate, and it had started to feel like we were forgetting our native language. We attended an international church, found multicultural community.

I planned to go back to the university a day earlier than Lisa, so on Saturday evening I packed my satchel and hopped on a motorbike taxi, asking the driver to take me to the train station. He dropped me off at a station that seemed different than I remembered, but it was certainly a train station. I already had my ticket, so I sat in a plastic bucket chair in the open-air terminal. I tried to decipher the signs on the walls to tell when my train would arrive. I knew from experience that trains normally ran an hour or two later than scheduled, so I was mostly unconcerned about the empty station.

An hour passed. The light faded and the first stars emerged. I was basically alone in the terminal, though I noticed men across the street. I hadn't seen a single train come through since I'd arrived, and it didn't look like anyone else was waiting. I must have made a mistake.

Embarrassed, I suddenly realized I must not have spoken clearly enough to the taxi driver. I should have recognized right away that this was the wrong station. And then I became afraid. It was dark, and I was alone—a small, twenty-two-year-old foreign woman. *God, please help me get back*, I prayed.

I walked until I found another motorbike taxi, and handed the driver a business card with Camille's address on it. I sat sidesaddle behind him, praying he would take me to the right place until I finally recognized the streets again, then saw Camille's gate. I paid the driver without haggling, just raising

my eyebrows to show him that I knew he was swindling me. Then I went back into the house, briefly telling my friends that I had gone to the wrong train station somehow, but that I would just go back tomorrow with Lisa after all. I escaped upstairs before I would have to answer any more questions.

For the first time I realized how vulnerable I was, how easy it would be for me to disappear. Typically, I traveled with the confidence of the young and privileged. We tend to believe we are invincible, moving with careless confidence, trusting the world as it comes to us, believing in the essential goodness of humanity. I'd shared sleeping quarters with strangers in hostels across Europe, taken solitary hikes in Switzerland, slept in train stations in Germany. I'd hopped into taxis alone and ignored the advances of the flirtatious men in French parks. I'd walked by myself down deserted Asian beaches.

I'd like to say that my confidence was founded on faith in God's providence, but that wasn't really it. It was simply that I was twenty-two, and I believed I was safe and strong. I believed in adventure.

That night, for maybe the first time, I was shaken by my naïveté, by what could have happened as the shadows lengthened. But back at Camille's, my fears dissipated quickly. Maybe too quickly. I could have used a dose of caution with what the rest of the year held for me.

Only a few weeks after our visit to the capital, Lisa and I traveled by train again, this time to a southern coastal town for a Thanksgiving celebration with the English teachers from our training class. I couldn't wait to talk about books with Camille, to swap CDs with the adorable Jack, and to chat with his energetic teammate Joanna.

Lisa and I woke before dark, having arranged for our usual motorbike taxi guys to meet us at the university's back gate at 3:30. As we trudged groggily down the stairs, a light rain began to fall. When we got to the back gate, we realized—of course!—that it was locked every night, and we couldn't get out that way. We scrambled to the front gate, but couldn't find our moto drivers anywhere and began praying as the rain fell more and more heavily. Finally we saw a man on a motorbike, and convinced him to take us to the train station. Both of us sat behind him, our backpacks hanging off to the sides of the motorbike.

We sighed with relief—we would make it, after all. Until the driver took us to a hotel. Our pronunciation was so bad that he didn't understand where we wanted to be. After the hotel, he thought we were asking to go to the chicken market, and he showed us that it was closed. Finally the lightbulb switched on; after we repeated the word for "train station" two dozen times with various inflections, he got it and smiled broadly. We made it to the

station with five minutes to spare, only to wait an hour for the train, which was, of course, late.

After a full day on the rocking train—nodding off on hard seats, waking to watch the countryside pass, eating packets of crackers and drinking warm Cokes—we finally arrived. The teachers who lived in this gorgeous, beachy town helped us get settled in at the Australian bed-and-breakfast on the water. They told us we'd already lost two members of the party; one of the teachers had been diagnosed with a bleeding ovarian cyst, and flown to a hospital in Bangkok. Camille had gone with her. Other teachers were still en route, so we had a quiet evening and went to bed early.

The next morning I woke as usual at six, and took my laptop out on the empty deck to journal while I listened to the waves. A few minutes later Jack came out.

"Hey," I said, smiling. "Did you just get in?"

"Yeah, we had an overnight train that got in about an hour ago. I thought I'd take a nap, but I can't sleep," he answered. He folded his lanky body into the chair next to mine and pulled out a novel by Zadie Smith. I typed quietly, pretending I wasn't buzzing with electricity at his proximity, just journaling and checking e-mail.

I hadn't heard from Charley in about a week. Getting him to actually write e-mails was sometimes like pulling teeth, and his last message had been despondent and whiny. When we finally chatted on instant messenger, he'd been evasive and defensive: "I'm afraid you're angry at me," he'd written. "I know I haven't e-mailed. I have the usual excuses. It's been a hard week. I'm afraid of teaching my class tomorrow. I'm not getting along with my team-mates, except Cady." We *had* to communicate if we wanted a relationship, I told him.

Charley:	I'm afraid of our relationship.
Amy:	I don't know what that even means.
Charley:	. . .
Charley:	I know that we need to talk about things, but it just takes so much emotional energy that I don't really want to do it.
Amy:	Okay.
Charley:	Do you think this is good?
Amy:	What do you even mean? I don't know what things you think we need to talk about! If you do want to say something, then

say it. But if you don't, I'm not going to sit here encouraging you to share your emotions if you don't think you have the energy to do so. Either be in this relationship or be out of it, but don't ask me to beg for it!

Charley: See, that's what I mean.

I wondered what he wanted to talk about: Did he need reassurance that I cared for him? Or did he need to confess something? Had he kissed Cady? I was tired of dealing with him, of dealing with our relationship. I put in my earbuds and watched the waves. Jack and I settled into a companionable silence until the others came down.

That weekend we all took long walks on the beach, swam, clambered over rocky cliffs. We feasted: roast chicken, mashed potatoes and gravy, stuffing, canned cranberry sauce, green beans, carrots, bread, and even pumpkin pie. We went around the table saying what we were thankful for. I talked about Veronica. We sang hymns and praise songs with an acoustic guitar, then stayed up until two in the morning playing raucous card games.

8

• • • • •

The Backstreet Boys
and Salvation

Human nothingness, divine sufficiency.

from *Hudson Taylor's Spiritual Secret*

As Christmas approached, the weather was far from frightful, no chance of snowmen or sleds in our future. Temperatures hovered in the seventies during the day, and overnight our rooms, not equipped with heaters, just barely began to feel chilly. One bookstore in town had a picture of Santa in a window, but other than that, there was no sign that we were in either the holy season of Advent or the commercial season of Christmas.

I was feeling farther and farther away from my life in America, like I was existing in some other realm, outside of time altogether. But it wasn't homesickness.

Life had begun to feel almost normal. In the mornings I woke up early and plugged away at the book I was writing, a catalog of all the ways the church in America had adopted American cultural values instead of holding to true scriptural faith. Lisa and I taught our classes, hung out with students, took motos over to our favorite restaurant for fried rice, and watched *The West Wing*. On Sundays we went to the beach with Tina and her friends or

other groups of students, walking in the surf, ordering fresh-caught crab, and eating under a beach café tent.

I'd been so warmly welcomed from the time I arrived in the city that I'd started to feel at home here, at ease. I was beginning to admit to myself that I didn't *want* to go back to America when my year of teaching was up. I wanted to stay another year, or longer. Maybe forever.

I guess it was the sense of safety I felt that allowed me to forward the e-mail. One morning in my in-box, I read a horrifying account my mom had sent me from the Voice of the Martyrs. A witness spoke of dozens of Christians from a minority tribe murdered by police in the hills of my country. I could hardly believe it—here, in this hospitable country, among these warm, caring people? I absently forwarded the message to several other teachers in the country, adding "Something to pr about." We used abbreviations for explicitly Christian words like *pray*, knowing it was likely that government programs scanned all e-mails for certain "high alert" words.

A response came back swiftly, a reply-all e-mail from Camille. In terse language and no uncertain terms she scolded me for sending an unverified report that did not honor our gracious hosts. I instantly realized what I had done. I'd somehow remembered to abbreviate "prayer" without even thinking about the content of the rest of the e-mail. I'd compromised not only myself, but every other teacher I'd sent it to.

Mortified, I apologized. Camille sent me a private message explaining that she needed to respond harshly just in case anyone was reading our correspondence, but that I did need to be more thoughtful. We had communication guidelines that we were supposed to follow. I had to force myself to remember, despite evidence to the contrary, that this beautiful, warm country was still dangerous—for me and others.

I closed my computer and hurried to my writing class, struggling to ignore the weight that felt like a boulder on my chest, the sense of personal failure. Four students came in late, neglecting to duck their heads and say "Sorry, teacher," as they entered. They were effectively disrespecting me, and another group failed to pay attention as I spoke. I snapped at the class, telling them to open their notebooks and free-write in silence for ten minutes. Then I turned to face the board, winking back tears.

I was a failure as a teacher, a missionary, a Christian. I walked slowly up and down the rows of desks, looking at the students' writing. One had passed a note to another, in English: *Miss Amy seems cried*, it said. I pushed my feelings of inadequacy away. "You can put your notebooks away for now and open your textbooks," I announced, calmly taking my place at the front of the class.

• • •

My despondency faded as the sun set. I knew that the heaviness I felt was not really about fear or guilt or worry; it was simply that my pride was hurt. I hated making mistakes, especially public ones, especially in front of Camille, whom I adored. I hated being wrong. I confessed my pride and self-righteousness to God, and tried to get on with the work in front of me.

Veronica was coming over that night. We'd almost finished our study of Luke, and she'd been reading other parts of the Bible on her own, too: some of Genesis, all of Mark, and her favorite, Ecclesiastes. Her responses were inquisitive and emotional. "I don't understand why the disciples left Jesus in the Garden. Why did they run away? The story doesn't say, but it doesn't seem right!" She wrote her own poems in response to the lyrical verses in Ecclesiastes, and she told me that she was praying to God for help in her life. Once I had shown her a diagram that I'd been taught, long ago, depicting humans and God separated by a chasm. I'd explained that humans were created to be with God, but our sin had separated us from him. The result of our sin was death, but God loved us and sent Jesus to die in our place. I drew the cross in the chasm, making a bridge from humans to God.

As we studied together, I always tried to answer her questions and ask some in return. I never suggested that she invite Jesus into her heart, or confess her sins, repent, and submit to the Lordship of Christ. I never told her that she could pray a prayer and be assured of eternity in heaven. I never asked her if she knew what would happen to her if she were to die tonight. I disliked those forms of evangelism, but I also felt the cultural dynamics were too tricky. In this culture, students were expected to say yes to whatever teachers, or their elders, asked. Sometimes I'd invite students to come over to watch a movie. "Can you come tonight? Around seven?" I'd say, and they'd smile and murmur, "Yes, I think maybe."

But they never came. I finally learned that when students said maybe, it was simply a polite way of saying no. They couldn't say no to me. I didn't think I should ask Veronica if she wanted to follow Jesus, because she'd feel pressured to say yes, whether she meant it or not.

But that night as we wrapped up our study, Veronica said to me, "This is true, isn't it?"

"What?" I asked.

"I know this story is true. But I'm not good enough to be a Christian," she said.

We sat facing each other on the woven mat on my apartment floor, our plate of pear slices and cups of green tea forgotten. I looked at her thoughtfully,

and asked her to tell me what about the story she thought was true. Veronica had fire in her eyes. "God loves us," she said. "God loves us even though we don't deserve it. Jesus really lived, and died, and rose again. What Jesus said in this book is the most beautiful way of life I've ever heard of," she insisted. "I can never live up to it."

I looked into her serious, troubled eyes, and felt a smile creeping into the corners of my mouth. "Veronica, if you believe that, you already are a Christian. You're already part of the family of God."

We both paused. Joy and disbelief exploded across her face. "Really?" she said. She couldn't stop smiling. Normally melancholy, even cynical, now her face opened up.

"Yeah. You don't have to be good enough to be a Christian. You only have to believe in Jesus, in God's grace and love for you, and the Holy Spirit will come into your life and begin to change you. You already believe. That's all God asks."

We talked more, and we both prayed. Veronica hugged me and left, and I could tell by the look on her face she was treasuring up all these things in her heart, and pondering them.

I knew Veronica was coming to faith with a variety of motivations, including her obsession with pop stars who claimed the name of Christ. She already felt like an outsider and a failure in her culture, and had come to me looking for something to belong to. But I also knew she hadn't done anything out of a desire to please me. She truly had been captured by Jesus's vision of another way of living, and she had fallen in love. I hoped that Jesus, to paraphrase the title of a Backstreet Boys song, wasn't playing games with her heart.

9

. . . . .

Christmas Parties

I had a really delightful time teaching the children [I had just met], both boys & girls, out of the catechism. Then I made them repeat after me the first stanza of "Happy Land" & sung it over with them many times.

Lottie Moon, February 25, 1876

Lisa and I hosted parties in our apartments every night during the week leading up to Christmas. One by one, we had our classes over for some traditional holiday cheer. On Monday evening around seven, Tina brought the first students to my room, where they sat cross-legged in a big circle on the floor. Girls leaned together, and boys put their arms around each other, normal gestures of same-sex friendship. Tina stayed a full foot away from her boyfriend, an older guy whom she'd brought to the class party so we could meet him. He looked awkward behind his glasses, and Tina seemed particularly ghostly. She'd been applying a face-whitening cream many Asian women used to look "more beautiful," and she looked like she'd lost weight. I passed plates of gingersnaps and sugar cookies in her direction, but she just handed them on.

Grabbing the guitar, I led the students in a Christmas carol, and then Lisa read what we called "the Christmas story," Luke 2, explaining that it's the reason we celebrate this holiday. Imagine that you know nothing of the

Christian faith, that you've never heard of Jesus, and someone tells you that the biggest holiday in her country commemorates this story:

It was about that same time that Augustus Caesar sent out an order to all people in the countries that were under Roman rule. The order said that everyone's name must be put on a list. This was the first counting of all the people while Quirinius was governor of Syria. Everyone traveled to their own hometowns to have their name put on the list.

So Joseph left Nazareth, a town in Galilee, and went to the town of Bethlehem in Judea. It was known as the town of David. Joseph went there because he was from the family of David. Joseph registered with Mary because she was engaged to marry him. (She was now pregnant.) While Joseph and Mary were in Bethlehem, the time came for her to have the baby. She gave birth to her first son. She wrapped him up well and laid him in a box where cattle are fed. She put him there because the guest room was full.

That night, some shepherds were out in the fields near Bethlehem watching their sheep. An angel of the Lord appeared to them, and the glory of the Lord was shining around them. The shepherds were very afraid. The angel said to them, "Don't be afraid. I have some very good news for you—news that will make everyone happy. Today your Savior was born in David's town. He is the Messiah, the Lord. This is how you will know him: You will find a baby wrapped in pieces of cloth and lying in a feeding box."

Then a huge army of angels from heaven joined the first angel, and they were all praising God, saying,

"Praise God in heaven,
and on earth let there be peace to the people who please him."

The angels left the shepherds and went back to heaven. The shepherds said to each other, "Let's go to Bethlehem and see this great event the Lord has told us about."

So they went running and found Mary and Joseph. And there was the baby, lying in the feeding box. When they saw the baby, they told what the angels said about this child. Everyone was surprised when they heard what the shepherds told them. Mary continued to think about these things, trying to understand them. The shepherds went back to their sheep, praising God and thanking him for everything they had seen and heard. It was just as the angel had told them.

Without any context, it doesn't make much sense, does it? Who is Quirinius? Why do these people need a savior? Why did angels appear to shepherds? Is this an old folk tale no one believes is *literally* true, like the folk tales our students told of their annual festivals?

Whether the story made sense or not, telling it was a way for us to check a safe "evangelism" box in our minds, something we could point to and say, "See? We really are doing what we're supposed to be doing here." Anyway, I thought of Gladys Aylward: one of her chief methods of evangelism was to tell stories, like that of Noah's ark, to the overnight guests at the inn she ran in China. If she did that, surely I should do this. I told myself that God promises, in a deep King James voice, that *his word shall not return void.* Doesn't that guarantee that any time we share words from the Bible, we will see some sort of . . . results?

Growing up in the church, I'd heard that phrase a lot—"his word shall not return void"—but I didn't quite know where it came from. Later that night I looked it up.

It's from Isaiah 55, a chapter in which God speaks to his special chosen people, the nation of Israel. God promises grace to his people, and deliverance from exile. It's in this context that he says, in verses 8 through 11:

> "For my thoughts are not your thoughts,
> > neither are your ways my ways,"
> > > declares the LORD.
> "As the heavens are higher than the earth,
> > so are my ways higher than your ways
> > and my thoughts than your thoughts.
> As the rain and the snow
> > come down from heaven,
> and do not return to it
> > without watering the earth
> and making it bud and flourish,
> > so that it yields seed for the sower and bread for the eater,
> so is my word that goes out from my mouth:
> > It will not return to me empty,
> but will accomplish what I desire
> > and achieve the purpose for which I sent it."

All I'd ever heard in these verses was a promise that if I shared the Word of God, I'd see some result. The other parts—the specific context about deliverance from exile, the acknowledgment of the mysterious and confusing ways in which God works, or the fact that God's words will accomplish what *God* desires, not what I expect—I'd never heard a sermon on them.

In any case, once we'd shared the story of Jesus's birth, the students took over the party. The gingersnaps languished in a corner while we snacked on

shrimp crackers and sour green mango dipped in spicy salt. The adorably dimpled Minnie, who gave me my cat Éponine, sang a traditional song, and everyone clapped; then they sang an old folk song together. Finally Tina gave a barely discernible nod, and immediately all the students stood up, saying, "I think maybe we should go now," scrambled back into their shoes and crowded out into the hallway.

By the time Christmas arrived, Lisa and I were exhausted from so much entertaining. The university didn't recognize the Christmas holiday, but Lisa and I did get the day off, according to a stipulation in our contracts. I woke up early and checked my e-mail. My parents had sent me an iTunes gift card. It took an hour or two to download each song on our internet connection, but I was happy for the chance to get new music. Then I hopped back in bed with a novel and read for two hours. As I was getting dressed around 8:30, there was a knock at my door. Three students stood in the hallway, one bearing a white slip of paper for me. There was a package waiting for me at the post office!

It seemed too good to be true—we were really getting a package on Christmas day?—but we skipped breakfast or coffee, and Lisa, Tina, and I hurried to the International Relations Office. There I could get the appropriate stamps allowing me to receive mail, then we were off to the post office to pick up the package.

The woman behind the counter asked me for money, about seven dollars, to release the package to me. Was this a bribe? Probably, but behind the counter was a cardboard box the size of a computer monitor from 1987, and I didn't care. I passed the colorful slips of paper money over the desk, and she handed me the cumbersome package.

It was from China, and the postmark was two months old. Back in my room, Lisa and I wondered how long it had been sitting in the post office waiting for us, if it had already been opened, if the post office workers had found anything inside that they couldn't live without. We opened it and found a letter on top:

Dear Amy and Lisa,

Our team of teachers in Changchun has decided to adopt your team! Since we can buy a lot of things here that you might not be able to get, we're sending you this care package. We're also praying for you! We hope your year is going well, and that you're seeing the fruit of your work!

Love,
Team Changchun

Charley's team in China had sent us a package, and I was suddenly in love again. We had DVDs, CDs, M&Ms, Strawberry Shortcake coloring books and crayons, all kinds of things silly and delicious and foreign and fun. Charley may have been uncommunicative lately, but the package assured me that he had been thinking of me. Everything was going to be okay. I couldn't wait until I saw him, in just four weeks, at our mid-year conference in Thailand.

Lisa and I decided to spend the day together. A package from my parents had arrived a few weeks earlier, with Reese's, and breakfast treats, and packets of taco seasoning, so we opened up the S'mores Pop-Tarts for our Christmas morning breakfast, sat under the small artificial tree that previous teachers had left for us, and exchanged presents.

Later, Lisa and I put on our nicest skirts and walked under a sunny, blue sky in 78-degree weather to the one fancy hotel our town boasted. We couldn't think of any other way to treat ourselves, so we visited the hotel restaurant, the only place in town where our meal might cost upwards of ten dollars. We sat shivering in the air-conditioned, vast and empty hotel restaurant and ordered everything we wanted: sweet corn soup, stir-fried squid, chicken, spring rolls, fried coconut cakes, and rice. We walked back at one, and the town was hot and silent, with everyone taking their post-lunch naps.

We called our families briefly. I missed mine, but I didn't feel sad, exactly. It just didn't feel like Christmas; I couldn't imagine that, a world away, it was cold and festive, everyone singing carols and opening stockings and clutching hot cocoas. Actually, I was feeling happy—happy to be walking through a quiet town, sweating lightly in my swishing skirt, heading up the stairs to watch a movie on a laptop on my day off.

10

......

Solos at Karaoke

He seemed to "realize always that he must be about his Father's business, and not wasting time in the pursuit of amusement."

said of William Borden, Yale graduate
who hoped to be a missionary to China
but died of spinal meningitis before arriving there

Classes resumed on December 26. Our break between semesters was not Christmas break, but Lunar New Year break, which began in early January and lasted for five weeks. All the students would visit their ancestral villages, spending the week before the Lunar New Year cooking, preparing foods to offer to visitors on New Year's Day. On New Year's Eve they would deep-clean their houses, sweeping out all the dirt and evil spirits and detritus of the old year. On their New Year's Day, they would receive gifts of money in red envelopes and new clothes; wearing their new clothes, they would walk from house to house in the village, visiting friends, relatives, and teachers.

But January 1 was nothing special in this country, so I scheduled a make-up session for Veronica's class that morning. They needed a full review before exam week began, and I wanted to make sure they got it.

The weather had started to seem cold, staying grey and drizzly for days on end. A damp fifty degrees, in rooms without heating, left me chilled, so

I wore a sweater and khaki pants to the make-up class Saturday morning at 7. I'd grown fond of this class: not just Veronica and her best friends Sarah and Cecilia, who also studied the Bible with us occasionally, but all of them. Henry, with big hands and eyes, the shy son of a farmer, wrote delicate poems about nature. Hallie, the pudgy girl in the front row who couldn't understand a single word I said, but smiled constantly, her eyes nearly disappearing when she did. She could speak only a word or two of English, but wrote me adoring notes filled with love. The class monitor, John, was a mischievous, confident boy more likable than leaderly. His girlfriend, a petite, smart girl with short black hair, was one of my favorite students. She asked to be called Avril, after pop singer Avril Lavigne, and everything about her seemed to quietly question her culture's status quo.

But none of these students were in the classroom when I arrived. Ten minutes later, a few showed up, apologetic, and we sat and waited for others. Finally, with less than half the class in attendance, I gave a halfhearted exam review. We ended early, and it felt like anything but a propitious way for the new year to begin. Gray skies, a failed make-up class, eight o'clock in the morning and a whole empty day stretching out in front of us. As we left the classroom, the monitor, John, invited us to go sing karaoke. Veronica and some others bowed out—karaoke was expensive, a rich kid's activity—but John's group of friends accepted his invitation, so I did, too.

Twenty minutes later, I was sitting on one of the sofas lining the perimeter of a small, dark room. John had rented this room for an hour, which meant we could choose our own songs, pass the microphone around the sofas, and sing along to the words on the TV screen in the corner. We could order shrimp chips, bottles of water, and cans of Coke. I'm sure if I hadn't been there, they would have drunk beer, too, but out of respect for me, they didn't.

This hour of karaoke cost John about three dollars, but his family was wealthy, and he didn't mind. We started with Abba's "Happy New Year," which I'd never heard before, but all the students knew it by heart and sang with gusto. They sang other, older American pop songs, by Lionel Richie and Michael Jackson, and pop songs in their own language. When my turn came, I chose Carole King's "So Far Away," and sang thinking of Charley and home.

It wasn't my first time at Asian karaoke. All of us teachers had gone during our training in the capital city. Second-year teachers Melissa and Erin were anxious to introduce us to the wonder of karaoke, and took us out one night to a nice place—black and red pleather couches, plenty of space. Melissa and Erin loved the spotlight: they not only sang "Dancing Queen," they danced it, too. I blushed when they tried to get me to choose a song, not confident

at all in my voice, not one of the popular, performing girls. "C'mon," Jack said, "I'll sing with you."

"I guess I could do something by John Denver," I murmured, and added "Annie's Song" to the list. I'd played it on my guitar before, and knew it was sort of in my range. When my song came up, I took one microphone and Jack took another.

Almost immediately I realized what I'd done. The words were incredibly romantic—about forests, sunsets, giving one's life away in love. I'd known this was a love song, I'd thought of that when I chose it—but I hadn't known how it would feel to sing it. I couldn't sing this song, not with Jack, who loved Flannery O'Connor, who'd lent me Damien Jurado and Gillian Welch CDs to copy onto my laptop, who in the taxi on the way over had shared three silly limericks he'd written about me. I could have sung it with another guy, with my brother, or mockingly, with my best friend, but I couldn't sing it with Jack—because it wouldn't mean nothing to me. I passed the microphone around the circle for someone else to take.

I'd been insecure about my singing voice, and I hadn't wanted to sing in front of anyone, regardless of whether the lyrics were loaded with meaning. But now, in a room with my students, I belted out the words to "So Far Away," and the karaoke machine gave me a score of 93 percent. I smiled and passed the mic to Avril.

With only nine days before I would leave for Thailand to take grad classes and attend our organization's annual conference, I began to pack and to dream. Lisa and I took Veronica out to dinner, and over spring rolls and stir-fry, we talked about her newfound faith. She wanted to know if she could keep my copy of the *Jesus* film while I was away—we'd watched it recently with Sarah and Cecilia, lying on our stomachs on my thin foam mattress, eating snacks. I told Veronica that she could keep it, but warned her that she needed to be careful. And I said that if she e-mailed me while I was gone, she should avoid certain words.

Veronica looked at me, something between pity and confusion in her eyes. "Amy, I've already told you that if I have to choose between my country and God, I choose God. And in the Bible it says that the Word of God is living and active, sharper than any double-edged sword. I have a more powerful weapon than my government does. I'm not afraid."

Lisa's head fell to one side, her mouth slightly open. I looked at her and quickly pulled my own jaw up, nodding at Veronica. "Okay," I said, and spooned some more fried pork onto her plate.

11

· · · · ·

Headless in Thailand

It is out of the question. I would never take the idea into consideration. I could not leave my work for such a reason.

> Mary Slessor, when her mission board asked her
> to leave her post if she wished to marry her fiancé

In Swaziland, Malla Moe was evangelist, church planter, preacher, and bishop. Back home in Norway, she was not permitted to speak in church.

> Ruth Tucker, *Guardians of the Great Commission*

In Thailand, the sun was always shining. In Thailand, there were places to eat bagels and strawberries and lasagna and avocados, things I hadn't seen in five months. In Thailand, there were big air-conditioned department stores in three-story shopping malls. I bought a swimsuit in one of those stores, and sat by the side of the YMCA pool eating chips and guacamole in the sun with Jack and Lisa, watching Charley do backflips off the diving board.

My grad cohort stayed at the Chiang Mai YMCA, along with our professors who had flown in from Chicago. We slept two to a room and ate breakfast together in the cafeteria, then moved to classrooms in the same building for instruction in TESOL Methods and Spiritual Gifts. On breaks, we'd go out

the back of the building to a convenience store across a quiet street and buy large cups of sweet, milky, Thai iced tea, the color of sunrise.

In our Spiritual Gifts class, I sat next to Rebekah, my companion for the master's program welcome dinner months earlier. "So, what's up with you and Charley?" she asked. Charley wasn't in our cohort—he, like Jack, Lisa, and several other teachers, had come to Chiang Mai early to hang out with us at the YMCA for the week before conference began.

"I don't know. . . . We're together, I think? We need to talk more. We need to see if we can make this work. It was a tough semester for us, and I think he's been depressed. He doesn't seem happy in China, but I really want to come back to Asia for another year, at least." I paused. "But it's so good to see him. It's really good to see him." I knew Rebekah wasn't Charley's biggest fan, so I changed the subject quickly. "What did you get on this spiritual gifts test?" I asked.

Before arriving in Thailand, we'd read a book that identified sixteen "spiritual gifts" mentioned in Scripture, claiming that understanding and developing our own spiritual gifts would be the most important work of our lives. I disliked the book, its clinical voice speaking of my spiritual life like a fish to be caught, cleaned, and gutted, dissected and divided—like the Bible was simply a handbook to be parsed. I had a hard time believing that when Paul made a list of spiritual gifts in a letter here, and another list there, he intended for us, hundreds of years later, to create one exhaustive list of gifts to be defined, codified, made into a quiz.

I was willing to believe, though, that I might be wrong, that maybe this kind of study of myself and my individual spiritual gifts could be something important. I had checked the boxes and counted up the results. Teaching, discernment, and apostleship were my primary spiritual gifts.

Apostleship confused me. The book explained that while the office of "apostle" had only been given to twelve—the original disciples minus Judas and plus Paul—the gift of apostleship was given to many. Apostleship was the gift of church planting, of leadership in "new works" of Christ.

But I was perplexed. If churches were supposed to be led by men, as I'd been taught my whole life, how could a woman have the gift of apostleship? Was it possible for me to preach the gospel to men? What was I supposed to do, start churches then put them on hold until a man could be found to preach? If Veronica was the beginning of a church in our town, what would we do when it grew?

The doctrines I'd grown up with—about gender divisions in church leadership—seemed to make even less sense outside the United States. What was

a female missionary to do? She could preach the gospel in evangelism, but once a church was formed, she was forbidden from preaching in the church pulpit? She could teach men about the Scriptures in small groups or one on one (or could she?), but not as head pastor of a church? And wasn't there something ethnocentric—even racist—in the American church's willingness to send female missionaries to preach and teach in foreign countries while refusing to let women preach or teach white American men?

But even as I began to doubt the theology of gender I'd grown up with, it continued to exert a powerful influence over my thinking about marriage. Choosing to get married, I was certain, would mean sacrificing my dreams to follow my husband's. I wasn't sure if I wanted a career or if I wanted children, but I felt sure that choosing one meant giving up the other. And I was convinced that I needed to marry a man who was a leader. I could only imagine him like the church leaders I'd grown up with—someone who loved the spotlight, who entertained an audience, who had more Bible verses memorized than I did, who knew more theological answers.

As Charley and I walked through the mall in Chiang Mai, we passed a jewelry store. I tried to imagine what I'd say if he proposed that week. I tried to imagine saying yes. I thought maybe I would say yes.

• • •

Conference was heaven. We stayed in a mountain resort, and every morning we'd gather, hundreds of us, a crowd of people of all colors and ages, the on-fire and the burned-out, Methodists and Baptists, Mennonites and Pentecostals, Yankees and Texans, Hong Kongers and Canadians, shoulder to shoulder singing "In Christ Alone." We listened to people teach from the Bible in our native language; we heard reports from teachers in every country of amazing things that had happened. We rested.

At dusk I'd sit with girls from my grad cohort in a gazebo, where we would read passages from Lauren Winner's *Mudhouse Sabbath* out loud to each other. After dark we'd gather around laptop screens and watch indie films on DVD. In the afternoons Charley and I would walk around the resort and find a clandestine corner for a kiss.

One afternoon he helped me with a project. My parents' church had asked me to record a message for a father-daughter Valentine's dinner. Charley borrowed a video camera, and I put on my pink button-down, found a well-lit spot in front of a lush green hedge, and began. I hadn't been given much instruction as to what the church wanted, so I decided to try to honor Dad

by speaking of things he'd done right as a father. Each of my three points told a story about him, then used Scripture to show how his practice of fathering was in line with God's design for dads. I drew on the small amount of Greek I knew from a class I'd taken in high school, the inductive Bible study skills I'd learned in college, and my natural gifting as a teacher. Telling stories and tying them to Scriptures, I exhorted the dads at the banquet to follow God's design and my dad's example.

When I finished, Charley turned off the camera, but didn't say anything. "Was it okay?" I asked.

"Is that what they wanted?" he asked in response.

"I don't know. It's for the father-daughter banquet," I answered, annoyed by his lack of enthusiasm.

"Yeah. You did fine, I guess," he said.

We took the tape out, returned the video camera to its owner, and slipped the recording into an envelope to drop off at the post office when the conference was over.

Perhaps Charley saw something that I hadn't. In attempting to honor my dad, I'd crafted a message that exhorted men, men who were older than I was. If I'd been thinking, maybe I would have written a message directed to the daughters. Instead, I'd told older white men what to do. I'd interpreted the Scriptures in a video that would be played in a conservative church in the south.

About a month later, the morning after the banquet, Dad called me. "How'd it go?" I asked enthusiastically.

"Not so well," he said. "Some of the men walked out." He paused. I was confused. Why did they walk out? Were some of the daughters wearing immodest dresses?

"They told me afterward that it wasn't right for you to be teaching the men like you were."

Silence deepened on the phone line, the eight thousand miles between our lives suddenly seeming more real than ever. Inside me, a door swung shut.

This church—not even a church I'd been a member of, not a church that financially supported me—had asked for a favor. I'd spent my free time and small missionary allowance to prepare and to mail the video. It had never occurred to me, when they asked me to record a message for the father-daughter banquet, that they wouldn't actually want a message. It hadn't occurred to me that they'd want me to craft a talk for a church event without using Scripture. It hadn't occurred to me that my dad would hear that kind of response without offering a counter-argument. But he himself had been taken aback by their response.

Anyway, this whole discussion, this question about "women's roles" in the church, was feeling increasingly irrelevant to me. The questions just didn't make sense halfway around the world, for believers in fledgling churches in countries where faith in Christ was forbidden. I would need to study it all again, but my experience overseas was leading me to think that the churches of my youth were getting something wrong in the way they understood Paul's instructions to Timothy, those comments about women being "silent" in the church.

I left the argument, tired of the words, hurt that my dad had to be the one to tell me what had happened. If the elders of that church really cared about me, they would have addressed it with me themselves, but they didn't. I never heard a word from them.

I left the argument, and drove my motorbike out to the beach, walked in the sand with my students, and ate freshly caught fish. I saw where the Spirit was moving, and I followed, needing no one's permission but God's.

• • •

Maybe we broke up because of that, because Charley saw women as "helpers" and "followers," men as "heads" and "leaders." Maybe we broke up because I loved my life overseas and he didn't love his. Maybe there were things about ourselves we hadn't admitted to each other. Maybe there were a thousand reasons, not just one.

After conference, Charley and I traveled with a group of our friends to a beach in southern Thailand, and then he came to visit my country for a few days, staying in the spare apartment in our building on campus. I knew that having Charley stay on our floor on campus might signal to the conservative local culture that I was, after all, a promiscuous American, just as they'd assumed from what they knew of Americans on TV. But I didn't care much about appearances—surely those who knew me would know better than to believe any gossip.

Charley ate with me at my favorite restaurant and came to dinner at Veronica's house. I rode the train back to the capital with him, and we spent two days there at Camille's before he caught his plane to China.

We talked to her about our relationship over dinner at the Australian burger joint, laid everything bare.

"It seems to me," she said, looking thoughtfully at me, her eyes crinkled with questions, "that if you want to come back here next year more than you want to be with him next year . . . that means something."

It didn't, though. I'd read numerous missionary biographies where people postponed marriage for years, refused proposals, and left their spouses, all in the name of evangelism. Love that overthrows life was Shakespeare (or maybe *Shakespeare in Love*), not Scripture. Certainly it was possible to love my work more than I loved my boyfriend, yet still love my boyfriend?

I turned her words, and my counter-arguments, over in my mind. Later, leaning against Charley on the blue sofa at Camille's, I said what seemed inevitable to me—and must have been to him.

"We can't keep doing this," I spoke softly. "I love you, but I don't want to marry you. We need to break up, for real this time."

I thought about the first time I'd seen Charley, in an honors English class our freshman year. I hadn't noticed his muscular calves or soft, full lips. I had noticed his shaggy hair and round nose, the way they reminded me of a brown bear cub. I'd noticed his wry smile and sarcastic wit. When in that Great Books class our text was Romans, he hadn't brought a printout to class like most of the other students—he'd brought a worn, leather-bound MacArthur Study Bible. I'd set my Bible on the desk, too, a secret signal saying *talk to me*. Soon he had stopped sitting in the back row, and moved up to the front row to sit next to me.

Now, at my suggestion that we needed to break up, he didn't argue. I think he'd known for a while how tenuous my love was. Maybe that's what he'd been afraid of—afraid to tell me real things about his life in case I was just waiting for an excuse, a good reason to break it off. My love was a kind of waiting, testing love, always uncertain of whether he deserved it. His friends in college had warned him that he deserved better than that, better than me, and they were right. Love should be unconditional, but mine always had strings. It was always waiting to see if he would be good enough, good enough for me to give up everything else for.

I let him go.

Interlude

Prior to about the 1820s, the word *missionary* was a male noun. There were missionaries, and there were missionaries' wives (though in the 1800s, that was a new thing, too—most missionaries up until then had been celibate males). But for a woman to be a missionary was against "the whole tenor of Scripture" and "out(side) of her sphere of duty," as a writer in *Christian Lady's Magazine* claimed in 1836. In the early Victorian period, women were to stay at home; they were the weaker sex, they were prone to fainting fits. They were angels or whores, but nothing in between.

In Victorian England, Christian women who felt a calling to something other than wifehood and motherhood had few options. Increasingly, though, women who wanted to work in the public sphere found more freedom to do so if they married missionaries and moved across the ocean. Overseas, missionary wives could do jobs that at the time were considered inappropriate for women in England or America.

Ann Haseltine was one who sought "a life of usefulness" and first made the role of "missionary wife" a legitimate calling for nineteenth-century American women. At twenty-three, she married Adoniram Judson, and two weeks later, they set sail for India, then Burma. They studied the local language and saw their first convert. During the first Anglo-Burmese War, Adoniram was imprisoned on suspicion of being a spy. For seventeen months, Ann lobbied for his release, living in a shack outside the prison gates, nursing a baby, and writing tragic descriptions not of her own plight, but of the way Burmese females were treated: the infanticide of baby girls, young girls being given in

marriage, status and human rights conferred on women only through their husbands.

After Adoniram's release, they stayed in Burma. Ann wrote a catechism in Burmese, and translated the biblical books of Daniel and Jonah. In 1819, she translated the Gospel of Matthew into Thai, the first time any Protestant had performed Bible translation into that language.

In the first half of the nineteenth century, women like Ann Judson were self-deprecating in the letters they sent back home. To maintain Victorian norms of domesticity, they masked their participation in traditionally male enterprises. But increasingly, they *were* doing more than keeping house overseas. After Ann Judson's death, Adoniram married twenty-eight-year-old widowed missionary Sarah Boardman, who was no shrinking violet. Sarah had chosen to stay in Burma after her first husband's death, and had taken over his work, making evangelistic tours through remote jungles, preaching the gospel to the Karen people, and supervising mission schools.

Around the same time, Betsey Stockton became the first unmarried female missionary sent out from America. A freed domestic slave, she traveled with a missionary couple, partly to serve them and partly to do mission work. In the Sandwich Islands, now known as Hawaii, she started a school for fishermen, farmers, and craftsmen.

More and more women, single and married, became active as missionaries in their own right. By the mid-nineteenth century, the word *missionary* no longer referred only to celibate males. Women began telling their own stories, too. *Memoirs of British Female Missionaries* (1841), collected by Jemima Thompson, was a kind of manifesto promoting female missionary endeavor, opening with a long essay on "the importance of female agency in evangelizing pagan nations."

Some men championed women on the mission field. Hudson Taylor welcomed single women to the China Inland Mission, sending them out two by two to the villages, praising their effective preaching. When Christian and Missionary Alliance members disagreed about women's roles in ministry, their leader A. B. Simpson said, "Let the Lord manage the women. He can do it better than you, and you can turn your batteries against the common enemy."

But sometimes women had to fight their agencies—and even their own husbands—to fulfill their callings. Lottie Moon, a Baptist missionary to China, saw more than a thousand people come to Christ as a result of her work. In early letters home, though, she wrote things like, "I halted at two villages and had an enjoyable time talking to the women. That the men chose to listen too was no fault of mine!" Later, she took a stronger stance:

"What women want who come to China is free opportunity to do the largest possible work. . . . What women have a right to demand is perfect equality."

Pearl Buck, author of the Pulitzer Prize–winning novel *The Good Earth,* grew up as the child of missionary parents in China. As an adult, she wrote about watching her parents negotiate their roles, describing her mother's realization that her husband, Andrew, did not believe in the priesthood of all believers, only in the priesthood of men. "What?" Buck wrote. "Was she not to go to God direct because she was born a woman? Was not her brain swifter, keener, clearer than the brains of most men? Why—was God like that, Andrew's God? It was as though she had come bearing in her two hands her rich gifts of brain and body, giving them freely and as touchingly sure of appreciation as a child—and her gifts had been thrown back at her as useless."

Women on the mission field made great strides, but still they struggled against patriarchal assumptions that undergirded some Christians' beliefs. Then, in the twentieth century, many of the female mission societies that had formed over the previous hundred years merged with general denominational mission boards. When they did, women typically lost their positions of leadership.

• • •

Historically, women on the mission field changed the Christian view of women's roles and women's spheres. Over about two hundred years, the church's position on women in ministry changed dramatically. Yet for many American Christians, a woman's place on the mission field remains limited to supporting roles.

When I was overseas, my ministry experiences didn't fit with the mixed messages I'd received about women in the church. My questions about the roles of women in missions multiplied.

What does it mean for a woman to be a missionary?

Can she be a nurse or a schoolteacher, but not a church planter?

Can she preach?

Can she teach men, or only women?

Can she teach brown-skinned men, but not whites, as if brown-skinned men are somehow less of men?

Can she lead a co-ed Bible study?

Can she lead a church?

If a man asks her how to be saved, can she answer him?

If he's never read the Bible, can she explain its meaning to him? Or should she say, "I'm sorry, I can't talk to you about what the Scriptures mean. I'm a woman. If God loved you, he would have sent a man whom I could support in this work."

The churches I grew up in wouldn't necessarily have endorsed that last line, but they agreed with the message at the heart of it. Women were not to teach men.

Or, if they did allow women to be church planters and Bible teachers on the field, they had a reason: women can lead churches on the mission field but not back home because of the extreme need on the mission field. Women can do it, they'd say, but it's "not God's best." They'd compare female missionaries to Deborah, whose good leadership of Israel they claimed was a "judgment" on Israel's men for not assuming leadership themselves. She was made judge over Israel, they said, to shame the men for being so lacking.

The thing is, the book of Judges never indicates that God viewed Deborah's leadership that way.

In the same way that female missionaries changed the church's perspective on the role of women in ministry, my experience as a woman on the mission field began to change my mind. It was this experience that first nudged me toward understanding that both men and women could be called to all kinds of service for God. Observing an Asian church in its infancy showed me how the systems and structures that had developed over centuries in the West were less biblical, more man-made. Living in and understanding another culture helped me see that much of what I thought it meant to be "woman" was culturally prescribed, not essential. Much of what the church had taught me about womanhood had more to do with customs—Victorian customs—than with Scripture.

But women like Ann Judson, Betsey Stockton, Lottie Moon, and Amy Carmichael showed me another way. A woman's vocation is her own, and not her husband's. And that's a truth that is always good for the church.

12

· · · · ·

Further Out

Mission begins with a kind of explosion of joy. The news that the rejected and crucified Jesus is alive is something that cannot possibly be suppressed. It must be told. Who could be silent about such a fact?

Lesslie Newbigin, *The Gospel in a Pluralist Society*

Placing my red satchel on the flat wooden desk, I organized my textbooks inside it as the freshmen filed out of the classroom. Veronica remained seated at her desk at the side of the room, waiting for everyone to leave. Then she came up to me.

"When can we study the Bible again?" she asked. "I have to tell you something. I have a plan."

I lifted my eyebrows. "Tonight?" I suggested.

That evening I made green tea and set some crackers on a plate. Veronica brought a tangle of rambutan, spiky-skinned pink fruits. I squeezed one until the skin broke, then peeled it and popped the translucent white flesh into my mouth, sucking and then spitting out the seed. Most of the food lay forgotten, though, as she began telling me the plan she'd devised while I was in Thailand.

"Amy," she said, "I have a plan to change the minds of my people. I will begin by telling my friends and family about what I have learned, and then

I will ask them what they think about it. I can show them the film that you showed me. And then," she said, "they will tell their friends and family, and it will be like in that movie *Pay It Forward*—the good news will spread all over! What do you think?" she asked.

I had to smile, seeing that a girl who had never been instructed to share her faith was bubbling over with desire to do so. It was a beautiful plan. She proceeded to tell me that it was already in motion.

"I showed my family the *Jesus* movie while you were gone. My father was angry when he watched it, and said it was not true. But then he watched it again. And again. He watched it four times, and invited our neighbors to come watch it with him. My father and the neighbor agreed that the film wasn't true."

While the men seemed unconvinced, Veronica's neighbor had said, "The people of our country don't know about this story, and they need to. Can I make a copy of the movie?" Veronica told him that her teacher wouldn't permit it—but he made a copy anyway. Then he took it to his ancestral village, and everyone came out to watch it.

Worry tinged my wonder at Veronica's story. She needed to be more careful, but what could I say? The last time I'd warned her she'd quoted Scripture at me. Maybe my fear, not her zeal, was the real problem.

The following week, I went to dinner at Veronica's house. I sat on a woven mat on the floor, knees together, feet tucked neatly behind me, as did Veronica, her parents and younger brother, and the neighbor who had watched the *Jesus* film. We served each other food from communal bowls. I liked this cultural tradition: we never served ourselves, only each other, always trying to honor someone else with the choicest pieces of meat, always tuned in to whose bowl was nearly empty and filling it with rice. At each meal, we took a bite of rice first, to respect the food that brought their ancestors through times of famine.

As we finished eating, Veronica began to translate for us. The adults wanted to talk about Jesus, but they began by saying what a sacrifice it was for me to come to their country. I protested—I loved their country and was happy to be there. It wasn't a sacrifice.

"It is a sacrifice," Veronica's dad insisted. "The Holy Spirit must have led you here."

"Yes," I nodded, shocked by his casual mention of the Holy Spirit. "That's true."

"My neighbor says that he wants more details about the film," Veronica translated. I agreed to get him a copy of the book of Luke in his own language.

"He says he's not convinced that the film is true," Veronica continued. I didn't try to convince him, just nodded. Since they had already invoked the Holy Spirit, I figured I could, too.

"Maybe the reason you're so interested in the film is that the Holy Spirit is calling you," I suggested. Even I could understand his response: he nodded, saying basically, Yes, I think that's true.

As the sun went down, Veronica gave me a ride home on the back of her motorbike. She came inside to pick up the book of Luke for her neighbor, and then hugged me good-bye. It would be so much easier, culturally, for her to keep following Jesus if her parents also came to faith. I prayed that they would.

Veronica and I continued studying the Bible together every Sunday night, and she regularly told her best friends, Sarah and Cecilia, what she had learned. Finally, they both decided that they wanted to study the Bible, too, so I began an introductory study with them on Monday nights. Sometimes all four of us would zip around town on their motorbikes, stopping to eat a favorite local snack: tiny pink shrimp, encased in a translucent gelatinous rice dumpling, topped with fresh herbs, chilies, and crispy fried onions. I grew to crave it.

Veronica would call me on the phone when she was reading the Bible. Once she called me after reading Romans 5. "Amy, this is so wonderful!" she said. "This letter—a letter of Paul, right?—has so many beautiful things. He really understood the gospel. I feel so wonderful! Sometimes I call my friends when I read something like this, but they never understand why I'm excited. I just had to call you."

Another day, after she'd used a devotional she picked up at my apartment, Veronica called to tell me that the words of the prayers in the book expressed her feelings exactly. "And I don't know if this is right or okay, Amy, but I feel that God is inside me and around me all the time. Is that okay?"

She'd read Mark, Luke, Romans, 1 and 2 Corinthians; large parts of Genesis, Exodus, the Psalms and Proverbs, and all of Ecclesiastes. Sometimes she copied out pages of Scriptures for her friends when they were worried or stressed. Her best friends from high school, who were attending universities in other cities, received letters filled with Scriptures. For an assignment in speech class, she was considering giving a speech about the gospel.

When Veronica began to vocally question the teacher of her government class, bringing her Bible to the classroom and reading it while the teacher lectured, I reprimanded her softly. She needed to be more careful. One night Veronica asked me why I hadn't told any of the third-year students, who had much better English ability, about Jesus. I told her that I'd had spiritual

conversations with some of them, but they hadn't shown interest. Still, I felt vaguely guilty. Should I have been doing more?

But I was doing a lot. The second semester seemed to pass much more quickly than the first, my days crowded with teaching, tutoring, language lessons, Bible studies, and reading for my grad classes. Anxieties about my own identity—whether I wanted a career or marriage, what kind of adult I was going to be—dissipated once I'd made my decision to return to teach another year. I began to see myself living long-term in this country, so even though cultural differences sometimes irked me—the campus loudspeakers beginning their songs and announcements at 5:45 a.m., for example, or the English faculty fatalistically sure that no change in their teaching methodology would make any positive difference for the students, or the university assemblies where everyone in the audience chatted throughout the president's speech—a sense of contentment, more than anxiety, began to characterize my days. Veronica had helped me understand my identity: I was a messenger, and a Bible teacher. Maybe that was enough for now.

I began exploring new parts of the town on my bike by myself, buying notebooks in a bookstore, trying a coffee shop—a real one, not a plastic stool on the hot sidewalk, but a place with normal sized tables and air-conditioning. But I wanted to go farther. I wanted an electric motorbike.

Our organization's policy was that first-year teachers could not own motorbikes. But I convinced Camille that an electric motorbike was a different category, something between "bike" and "motorbike," and that since I had signed on to return for another year, I was almost a second-year teacher already. She smiled, and I went to the ATM to take out two hundred dollars.

Tina took me shopping the next day. I trusted her to be a fair cultural broker. She'd have to negotiate a good price for me as well as a good price for her friend who was selling. We settled on a maroon motorbike with space-age curves. It was practically a toy, only accelerating to 40 kilometers per hour (about 25 miles an hour), and the fully-charged battery would allow me to travel about 50 kilometers (30 miles) before I'd need to plug it in again.

In the parking lot of the shop, Tina laughed at me as I tried out the motorbike for the first time. I wore grey dress pants that a local tailor had made for me, and a button-down and cardigan. I wore Birkenstock sandals, totally culturally inappropriate (I should have been wearing pointy-toed flats or feminine sandals with heels), but I was never able to give up my footwear. I donned a helmet and awkwardly, in fits and starts, drove in circles, smiling like an idiot.

I bought the motorbike even though I didn't have a place on campus to keep it. There was a storage room on the first floor of my building that would

probably work, but the first floor was a few steps above ground level, and there was no ramp. I'd learned by now that if I requested a ramp to be built, I'd hear, "Yes, sure"—and then nothing would ever happen. But I figured if I bought the bike, the university might feel more compunction to follow through. Until then, I stored my purchase at Tina's house. Since her dad was an administrator at the school, I hoped he might help push the project through any red tape.

Two weeks later, the ramp was built. Veronica gave me a ride to Tina's home, a big house out in the country. I brought flowers for Tina's parents, and we all sat in their front room, eating mangoes from their trees and drinking water. Tina translated for us, assuring her mother that the weather was indeed suitable for me here (even though I looked so thin), and assuring her father that she and Veronica would both follow me back to campus since it was already dark. I told Tina's parents that they were taking care of me just like my own parents would—a way of thanking them without saying thank you. In this culture, to say thank you was rude: you only thanked people you didn't have a relationship with. Instead of thanking friends, you simply acted reciprocally; they took you out for yogurt, then you took them out for yogurt. They watched your motorbike for you, and you brought them flowers.

Back on campus, we realized the ramp had been built in a corner without enough room to angle the motorbike onto it. Together, we managed to get the machine up, but I doubted I'd ever be able to do that on my own. I rolled my eyes at the world, and said good night to Tina. Veronica came upstairs with me.

"You seem too tired to study tonight," she said. "Let me rub your shoulders." We sat on the bed as she worked the tension out of my back. She told me about a book a Catholic friend had given her.

"The book says that Catholics care about history, tradition, and ceremony, and Protestants just follow the Bible. Is that right?" she asked.

"That's probably a reasonable way of understanding the differences," I agreed. Veronica said that the emphasis on ceremonies like confession didn't seem to fit with what she'd read in Paul's letters: he stated that in the past, people had to offer sacrifices, but since Jesus was the final sacrifice, we didn't need to offer them anymore.

Sometimes I wondered if Veronica needed my help at all.

13

. . . . .

Deeper In

As you wend your way from village to village, you feel it is no idle fancy that the Master walks beside you.

Lottie Moon, May 10, 1879

My phone rang on the first day of April.

"Amy?" said Veronica. "I have to tell you something." Something in her voice made me nervous.

"What is it?" I asked, worried. She paused.

"I have cancer of the liver," she said finally, her voice sounding choked.

"What?" I couldn't believe it. What kind of quack doctor had she seen? This couldn't possibly be true. And if it were, we would find a way to get her the best care. Surely this wasn't—

"April fools!" she cried.

Everything happened fast that month. One weekend I traveled with Sarah and Cecilia to Sarah's home, in a coastal village a couple of hours from the university. We met up with her high school friends, walked down bright streets under umbrellas to shade our skin from the sun, went to the beach and played in the water in our clothes—no immodest swimsuits for us. Sarah's mother cooked for us, roasting small birds over an open fire in the yard. I ate them, feeling tiny bones crunch in my mouth, and I ate the clams and

fried green vegetables, too. But I didn't try the stomach of the chicken or the heart of the pig. Sarah, Cecilia, and I slept spooned on a small wooden platform in one of the three rooms in the house. I woke around three to the noise of her mother preparing foods to sell in the market that morning, and went outside to pee in a hole in the ground.

A few weeks later, Veronica traveled to the capital with me for Easter, a holiday that most people in the country had no idea existed. At Camille's house, we met two dozen other locals on Saturday night to watch Mel Gibson's 2004 film *The Passion of the Christ*. I felt uncomfortable, though I couldn't quite put my finger on why. Didn't we all already know the story of the crucifixion? Watching this movie felt like we were emotionally manipulating ourselves. I found myself glad that it was just a poor quality DVD, with badly translated dialogue dubbed in, playing on a small screen.

As the story progressed, Veronica found me.

"I'm not sure I can watch this," she said.

"You don't have to," I agreed. "We can go into the other room." Instead, she sat in the back, sometimes averting her eyes from the screen, sometimes writing in her notebook instead of watching the film. She remained removed, at some level, from all the interactions that day, as if she was watching and testing the people there, waiting to ascertain how trustworthy they were. I wanted her to have Christian friends from her own culture, but I also recognized that this was just Veronica: always a bit of an outsider, analytical and passionate, hesitant to be a joiner.

Over dinner, though I couldn't understand the words, I watched her argue about the Bible with a boy who'd watched the film with us. Her eyes flashed, and I couldn't tell if she was excited or angry. Later Veronica told me that the boy knew of a house church just fifteen kilometers, about nine miles, from our university.

"Are you going to go?" I asked.

She laughed. "Are you really asking me that?" She glowed.

The next day, she attended a local church for the first time, later meeting a group of people in a public park for games, songs, and lunch.

Back in our city, we met for our weekly study. Veronica told me she had finished reading the whole New Testament, and that her friend Anna, whom I'd never met, had just finished reading the book of Luke. Anna told Veronica that, after reading, she believed in God and Jesus, but she wasn't sure if she wanted to be a Christian. Veronica planned to continue studying the Bible with her.

The very next weekend, Veronica, Sarah, and Cecilia traveled back up north for a retreat planned by one of the local Christians Veronica had met at

Easter. I rode the train with them, the four of us giggly, excited, and nervous to be traveling by ourselves. I wondered what their parents thought; the girls said their parents understood where they were going, and were okay with it. Not having enough language ability to communicate with their parents myself, I had to trust that that was true.

The retreat would be led entirely by indigenous Christians, mostly Philip, a twentysomething with a passion every bit as strong as Veronica's. Ten of them met in the capital and took another bus into the mountains, leaving us foreigners behind. I relaxed at Camille's house, reading her novels, going shopping for DVDs, working on my graduate school assignments. Camille took me to a jewelry store where I bought a necklace with the shape of our country dangling in silver from a chain, and we met with a small group of teachers to talk about what was happening in my city and how it might inform our work in other cities.

Finally, the girls returned. I met them at the train station so we could get back in time for school the next morning.

"Sarah and Cecilia are Christians now!" Veronica announced almost as soon as I saw them. I hugged the girls and murmured how happy I was for them. "We were all baptized," she added. Though flustered and pleased, I found myself immediately wondering if Sarah and Cecilia had felt pressured to do something they weren't ready to do. I wished they would have talked to their parents before getting baptized. But they appeared to be happy, and when I asked if it was what they had really wanted, they said it was. They seemed awed by the integrity, devotion, and love they'd seen exhibited by the others on the retreat.

On the train, as Sarah and Cecilia slept, Veronica crept into my sleeping bunk.

"I didn't agree with everything Philip taught," she confided in me.

"Really? Like what?" I asked.

"He taught us that if we follow Jesus, everything will work out in our lives," Veronica answered. "That we will be successful in what we try, that whatever we ask for in the name of Jesus we will receive, and we won't have suffering."

I didn't speak, wanting her to continue. She did.

"I told him, what about the first chapter of James? 'Consider it pure joy, my brothers, whenever you face trials of many kinds, knowing that the testing of your faith develops perseverance. And perseverance must finish its work so that you may become mature and complete, children of God.'"

I nodded. We stayed awake for a while, talking about the promises of God. God doesn't promise that life will be painless, only that we will never be alone in our trials.

The next month, our group of four began to grow. Nicole, who had read Luke and watched the *Jesus* film with Veronica, joined our Bible study. I talked about the truths of the gospel, and she said, "I really believe that. Since I read the Bible, I feel a new spirit that I never felt before. My mother has been reading it, too, and she wants to join us." Her face was radiant, and I think mine was, too.

Then Sarah brought her friend Tessa, and it seemed that every day someone new was interested in the Bible. I gave the girls resources, Bible study sheets and song lyrics, new blank journals, and instructions about how to go on meeting together and studying the Bible without me while I was gone for the summer. We went to a coffee shop, an empty, expensive coffee shop, and there they practiced having Bible study without me leading it—singing praise songs softly, reading Scripture, and praying together.

They were prepared for a summer without me, and I fully expected to return to a flourishing baby church.

14

· · · · ·

The Impossibility
of Self-Care

She seldom had time to cook proper meals for herself, and she was short of sleep too. At last her health gave way, and she was very reluctantly compelled to give up her slum work and take a rest.

Nancy E. Robbins, *God's Madcap: The Story of Amy Carmichael*

One of the secrets of going on is to get away. . . . Breathe sea air or mountain air or any kind of air that is pure and strong, and you come back refreshed.

Amy Carmichael, *God's Missionary*

Self-care, they told us in training, was essential to staying healthy when working cross-culturally. Drink enough water, get enough sleep, do the things that give you life. Treat yourself every now and then. Read your Bible. Be with people or be alone, whatever you need; get out of town at least once a semester. It doesn't sound like something the Heroes of the Faith would have done: they tended to work without ceasing, relying only on prayer to fill their wells, didn't they? Despite this, I tried to follow the advice.

In the fall Lisa and I had taken an overnight retreat to the beach, twenty kilometers (around twelve miles) from the university. We'd stayed in a new

hotel, painted a striking royal blue and hilariously named "The Green Hotel." (No, it was not particularly eco-friendly, either. The local language used the same word for green and blue—I imagine the English title was simply a poor translation.) With gleaming white tile floors, fresh seafood served on the patio, and air conditioners in the rooms, it was glorious, and less than twenty dollars per night. We took walks on the beach, posing for pictures next to old fishing boats, and we rented lounge chairs and read books and journaled.

Near the end of the spring semester, I needed to get out of town again. I'd been with people so much that my introverted heart was drying up, and I felt mentally and emotionally unprepared to go back to the United States. I wanted a day of silence. I wanted to ride my motorbike alone, feeling the wind in my hair, feeling free.

Maybe my wanderlust was coming back. When I got homesick, I got homesick for roads—for a stretch of highway at night, dark and lonesome through Mississippi, where once I'd stopped at a run-down four-pump station to hear a black man preaching the gospel out front. I got homesick for the road grey into Atlanta, snaking down to watch the sunrise over Highway 1 in Florida, the exhausted arrival at an all-you-can-eat breakfast buffet.

I missed the exhilaration of speeding down Long's Peak when the stars were out, those summers I worked in Colorado. Leaning forward on the dash, getting dizzy from the height and the curves and the night air rushing through the windows.

I missed the road north through America's heartland, erect grain silos staking the masculine territory, hand-painted signs calling down fire and brimstone on abortion doctors: a road so straight you could sleep and wake an hour later to the same wavy fields on either side, the same ribbon of black unswervingly stretching out in front of you. When the storms came, you could see them miles ahead—you'd watch the clouds gather and the color fade, you'd see the sheets of rain, like the curtain that was torn, long before you drove into them, drops plunking on your windshield. You saw through a glass dimly. You'd pull to the shoulder with your hazards on, listening to local radio, one station announcing which streets were closed, the other doing call-in song dedications, the voices so chummy you wondered if you belonged there, in that quiet town, two stoplights, eight hotels for the people halfway to Denver, halfway to someplace better.

What I had, though, was a twenty-kilometer stretch through rice fields, and little else. My backpack carried my laptop and journal, some pajamas, a clean pair of underwear, and two books to read. My bike was fully charged,

and I left early in the morning, before it got too hot. Halfway to the beach another motorbike pulled up next to me.

"Hello!" said the smiling woman.

"Hi," I replied with a plastic smile, trying to hide my annoyance. I was retreating, for crying out loud. I was trying to be alone, but everyone always wants to speak to the whiteskin blondhair.

"My name Leigh!" she exclaimed. "You American?" I answered yes, hoping the conversation would end quickly. And after another line or two, it did.

"Oh! That my house," she said, slowing to turn, and pointing to a small wooden house on a cement slab in a sea of rice plants and palm trees. "I invite you to my home!" she said.

I waved good-bye.

At the beach, I checked into a different hotel, this one only fifteen dollars per night, then went to sit on the beach and read. The book I was reading—for a grad class on leadership—argued that the development of Christian leadership followed a set pattern of three phases: Sovereign Foundations, Inner-Life Growth, and Ministry Maturing. I was supposed to chart my life on this graph, figuring out which lessons I had learned in each phase, and where I was now. The concept was silly, I thought, forcing my spiritual life into a formula. And following the instructions landed me solidly in the third and final phase. At the age of twenty-two. Which even I knew couldn't be right.

I sighed and put the book down, feeling restless. I had come here for spiritual renewal, for quiet time, but I felt fidgety, and God seemed too quiet. I tried to mentally prepare myself to go home, journaling answers to the questions people would ask me, making lists of the highs and lows of my year, lists of the things I was afraid of about the summer and the things I was looking forward to.

But I kept getting distracted, thinking about Jack. He had almost come to visit Lisa and me the previous weekend with his teammate Joanna, but ended up going camping with one of his classes instead. Joanna had come to visit, riding a slow train north to our town. It was enlightening to see our home through her eyes: she'd been shocked by how poor our area was.

Joanna taught with Jack and a young married couple at a university in the southern mountains, in a city that locals called the "city of love" because it was a popular honeymoon destination. They had nice restaurants, American food, a small expat community, lots of pine trees, even fields of strawberries (the rest of the country was too hot for growing berries). Our town was dusty and quiet, and our one western restaurant had just opened the week before Joanna arrived. We took her out to Halloween Pizza, where the walls were

mint green and hung with crucifixes, and MTV Asia played in the corner. High school girls at the table next to ours giggled nervously as they picked up bites of spaghetti carbonara on chopsticks. They looked like I had when I tasted sushi for the first time.

Joanna's visit lifted our spirits. She kept telling us stories about the funny things Jack said, hilarious adventures they'd fallen into trying to learn their way around their town. I'd wanted her to keep telling us those stories, because I was developing a deep, deep crush. Though I had always been an emotionally controlled person, never boy crazy, never having had a true secret crush on anyone, this time I just decided to indulge it.

I sent a gift for Jack back with Joanna, a copy of a mix CD my sister had sent me, guessing that he was as hungry as I was for new music after nearly ten months overseas. Jack e-mailed me the very day Joanna got home. He loved the CD, he said, and hoped he'd be able to see me over the summer while we were back in the States. We began a bantering, friendly e-mail correspondence. Did he know that I'd broken up with Charley? I hadn't said so; I didn't want to throw myself at him. But surely Joanna had told him? Right?

It was close to dinner time. I left my beach chair and returned to my hotel. Using hand motions and a little language, I communicated to the family who owned the hotel that my motorbike needed to be plugged in overnight. They nodded and nodded, and plugged it in. I went upstairs and tried to meditate on the Psalms in my room. Finally I put a DVD in my laptop and watched it in bed.

In the morning my feelings of restlessness and distraction continued. This retreat was a bust. No matter how many times I repeated words from Psalm 131 ("I have calmed and quieted my soul . . . like a weaned child is my soul within me"), my soul was disquieted. I hopped on my motorbike and headed back to the university.

Halfway home, I started losing speed. Soon I was crawling along at no more than 4 kilometers per hour, and I realized that the hotel proprietors had not, in fact, left my motorbike plugged in all night. It was out of juice. I cursed my lack of language skills and the local propensity to say yes when you meant no. Why hadn't they just asked for more money? I would have paid them to plug it in, if that's what they needed!

As my motorbike began to fail, I looked around. There was not another person in sight, just mosquitos and green, green heat. I was ten kilometers from town, and even if another person came by, it's not like they could bring me a gallon of gas. I didn't need gas, I needed an outlet.

And then I realized something: at the very moment my motorbike was dying, I was driving past Leigh's house. The woman who had introduced herself to me the day before lived right where I was, in the middle of this very rice field. I turned down the dirt path toward the home of the exuberant stranger I'd met briefly.

Leigh was happy to see me, and happy to let me plug into an outlet on the side of her house. Now that I saw her off of her motorbike, I realized she was pregnant, nearly full-term. She was probably only a few years older than I was. Leigh invited me to sit down, and pulled out a hairy coconut and a machete. Fascinated, and a little scared, I watched as this petite pregnant woman split the coconut in half and poured its juice into two glasses. She offered me one, and joined me at the table.

In broken English, Leigh told me what she could about her life. She'd married her high school "darling," who was traveling for his business now. She missed—no, not him—she missed the big city where they used to live, where she went to university. Her friends from college married foreigners and wrote her letters from Sweden and Canada. I gathered that she felt more like an exile than they did, sitting alone in this palm tree farm paradise. I worried about her, about what in my culture we would call depression, a disease that remained unnamed and undiagnosed in this country. I prayed silently for her.

After an hour, we'd exhausted our limited language capabilities. I thanked her profusely and hoped an hour of charging would get me the rest of the way home. But just within the city limits, still a kilometer or two from the university, my bike started to die again. I was ready to give up, praying, "Really, God?" As I puttered into town at slower and slower speeds, John, the freshman class monitor, rode up next to me. "Hello, teacher!" he said.

"John!" I was so relieved to see him. He was unfailingly cheerful and competent. "My battery is dying. What should I do?"

"Take my hand," he said, looking around for police. "I'll pull you." A couple of his buddies drove up on either side of us, blocking view of our illegal action from anyone who might be watching.

John pulled me all the way home.

"Self-care is not really working for me," I told Lisa later that night. We sat in our "kitchen," which consisted of an oven and a hot plate in the extra apartment on our floor. I scooped a last bit of scrambled eggs onto a bite of biscuit.

"What, you don't feel rested and refreshed after running out of battery power in the middle of a deserted road on a hot day?" she joked. We placed

our dirty dishes into a large plastic tub and took it into the shower in the back where we would wash them later.

"I wish I could take care of myself," I said. "I've always been independent."

"A little too independent," she observed. "Independence doesn't really translate here, though, does it?"

For our new friends, there was little concept of an individual apart from community. I couldn't imagine anyone emphasizing self-care to them. They wouldn't call it self-care; they'd call it community-care, maybe, if they named things like that. It would be about how understanding your place within a group can help you lead a healthy, happy life.

"I mean, self-care makes sense," I said. "I have to drink enough water and get enough sleep."

"But that's not really enough," Lisa said. "You wouldn't have made it home without Leigh or John."

As Lisa and I settled into our respective rooms for the night, I relished the quiet, my privacy, and my personal space. But I reconsidered my sense of my own self-sufficiency. Maybe that was an American cultural value that I had baptized in my mind as equal to responsibility or maturity. Though my culture praised independence, this culture valued interdependence, and I began to wonder if that wasn't actually the more Christian value.

After all, I couldn't take care of myself, especially in a place where I couldn't speak the local language. I was dependent on the kindness of both strangers and friends. I needed other people.

15

• • • • •

High Places
(Mistakes Were Made)

She wept many bitter tears and endured endless questionings as to whether
everything had been taken from her because of unfaithfulness on her part.

Henrietta Soltau, head of the
Women's Department of the China Inland Mission

And the high places of God's field call today for the love, and the zeal, and the
daring of those who will jeopardize their lives for higher ends.

W. H. Aldis, in a note sent out by the China Inland Mission in 1930

On my last night in the city, I crept out of my apartment after dark.
We lived on the top floor of the building, but I'd noticed that where
the staircase ended, there were iron rungs attached to the wall, leading up to
a hole in the roof. I could climb onto the top of the building. Campus was
mostly quiet, and I turned off the stairwell light before swiftly ascending.

I've always been attracted to heights. As a small child, I'd climb from my
bed to the top of my four-foot chest of drawers, sitting up there until my mom
found and reprimanded me. In the backyard, I claimed a tree as my own, nailing
an empty tin high up its trunk, keeping my secret papers inside. At summer

camp, at the age of eight, I used to rappel down the tallest towers, thrilled by the rush of adrenaline I'd feel as I jumped out, suspended over nothing. I'd flip and spin, doing tricks to impress the counselors.

In high school, I went to Haiti for a week. On our last morning in the country, my best friend, Mollie, and I woke up before daybreak and climbed out of our hotel window onto the roof. We took a box of dry cereal and a guitar, and watched Venus fade as a hazy, unspectacular sun rose over the colorful hills of Port-au-Prince. It wasn't really about seeing a sunrise, though; it was about sucking the marrow out of life, leaving conventionality and the plague of the mundane far behind. Those were very important things to do in the summer after tenth grade, when we were beginning to realize that pixie dust and feathers were no match for gravity, that carpets and elephants would never be able to fly.

In college I used to illegally climb the rusted iron fire escape on the side of Francis Hall, the building where my French classes met. I'd swing over the ledge and land lightly on the roof, then watch the stars, pray, and memorize Bible verses, rewarding myself with M&Ms.

I'd been wanting to get up on the roof of this building all year, but "unconventional" wasn't culturally lauded here the way it was back home. I had a sneaking suspicion that the university would not look favorably upon me hanging out on the roof. This was my last night, though. Up I went.

It was nearly midnight. The moon had been full earlier in the week, but was still big and yellow, hung low in the sky. I could see most of town: the student hostel across the street from my building, where many of my students lived; the lights of the bridge that led toward the ocean; the single light at the top of the mountain I'd climbed with Anne and Darcy, joking about finding boyfriends at the end; the hotel where Lisa and I ate seafood for Christmas dinner; the statue honoring the country's founder.

Summer lightning struck in the distance. I found the Big Dipper in the sky. But mostly I looked across the city, wondering what it would be like to go back to the States. Would it feel like home? Or would I feel like a flower picked from a garden and moved to a vase for ten months, then taken back to the garden and planted again, unable to re-root? I spun and spun on the roof, trying to memorize every sight as if I would never see it again. Ten weeks seemed too long to be away from this sweet place.

I had no idea, that night, that I would never come back. My motorbike would remain locked in storage, my clothes and books would languish in an empty room. I would never sing "Sweet Adoration" with Veronica, Sarah, and Cecilia again. I would never crack crab legs at our beach or fry cubes of pork in oil over a hot plate at a student's cement block apartment. I'd never again see Tina's

laughing eyes as she mocked the way I used chopsticks. I wouldn't be there when Anne and Darcy found the love they were searching for. I'd never read another of Henry's poems, or have another conversation with Avril about punk rock.

For months afterward—no, for years—I would catalog my infractions, the things that might have been the cause of what happened next. I still do it, catalog and flog. There were so many things I didn't know, so many things I took for granted, so many ways I wasn't cautious.

1. I shouldn't have forwarded that e-mail about the execution of Christians in our country.

2. I shouldn't have let Veronica keep the *Jesus* film over the mid-semester break.

3. I should have warned her more. I should have argued back when she told me that the Word of God was living and active, sharper than a double edged sword. I should have said, "Yes, but . . ." But don't argue with your philosophy teacher about politics. But don't lend my devotionals to your classmates. But don't make a speech about the gospel for a class assignment.

4. I should have been more tuned in to the other students. Were they jealous of my relationships with Veronica, Sarah, and Cecilia? Was I neglecting other friends for those three?

5. I shouldn't have let Charley visit the campus. He'd stayed down the hall, not in my room, but in this conservative culture, that looked bad enough. I'd only drawn more negative attention to myself by letting him come.

6. I shouldn't have taken the girls to that coffee shop for our last Bible study together. We'd sat on the second floor, the only customers there, and I thought we were safe. I thought it was a special celebratory ending to our year together. But we had prayed and read the Bible in public. Why had I been so foolish?

7. I shouldn't have let the girls go on that retreat without knowing more about it. I'd just trusted the teacher who connected me to those local Christians. I should have asked more questions. I should have been more careful.

I should have been more careful, I should have been more careful, I should have been more careful.

• • •

The word translated "high places" (*bamah*) is repeated 102 times in the Old Testament, mostly referring to Canaanite places of worship, altars on mountaintops and under "every luxuriant tree" (1 Kings 14:23). As I sat on the roof of my building that night, I thought about those "high places" and chuckled to myself, making little jokes about my penchant for high places, jokes that perhaps only the Christian-school educated would catch.

When the Israelites prepared to enter Canaan, Moses exhorted the Jews to "demolish all their high places" (Numbers 33:52). It was hundreds of years, though, before young King Hezekiah actually put an end to idol accommodation in Israel. Since the reign of Solomon, thirty kings (twelve in the southern kingdom of Judah, eighteen in the northern kingdom of Israel) had failed to remove the high places. But Hezekiah enlisted the help of the Levites and made sure the high places were destroyed, and that true, God-centered worship was restored in the temple (2 Chronicles 29–30).

The Jewish temple had a high place, a *bimah*, of its own, a raised pulpit from which the Torah was read. Scholars are unsure whether *bimah* derived from the Hebrew *bamah* or from the Greek word *bema,* meaning platform. Bema, when found in the New Testament, is usually translated "judgment seat." I used to hear pastors use the Greek word in sermons: "When you find yourself at the Bema seat," they'd ask, "what will Jesus say to you?"

It occurs to me now, as I rehash my mistakes, that what I'm doing is not what Jesus would do if I were to meet him at a high place.

It occurs to me now that obsessing over my own failures and what-might-have-beens is a way of creating my own altar, a *bamah* to me, a high place where I worship myself as the ultimate sovereign, responsible for whatever happens, good or bad.

Mistakes were made. I made mistakes. But obsessing over my mistakes elevates them as more powerful than the sovereignty of God. God is sovereign, and God is good, and God has forgiven me.

It would be at least a year before I was able to believe any of those things again.

. . . .

PART TWO

STRIPPED

But these strange ashes, Lord, this nothingness,
This baffling sense of loss?
Son, was the anguish of my stripping less
Upon the torturing cross?

Amy Carmichael

16

· · · · ·

Home

I have had a very pleasant time here—a number of calls and several invitations out.

Lottie Moon, at the end of her first home leave

It was one a.m. in Los Angeles, which meant it was three a.m. in Arkansas, my final destination, and three p.m. in Southeast Asia, the home I had left. The next-to-last leg of my journey was delayed by storms in Dallas, and I was wide awake, sitting on the floor of the terminal, taking it all in.

First: I was sitting on the floor. Which meant the floor was fairly clean. No one had spit on it, or dropped ashy cigarette butts on it, or just walked in from streets where men were peeing on one side and spilling cheap beer on the other. No one found it strange for an almost twenty-three-year-old girl to be sitting on the floor. I was sitting on the floor.

Second: I was eating a chocolate chip cookie as big as my head. Because this was America, where everything is super-sized and we don't think desserts are "too sweet"—the more sugar, the better.

Third: I was not the only white person in the room! In fact, there were people of all colors, sizes, and shapes here: tall white men with handlebar mustaches and cowboy boots; black, white, and Hispanic teenage girls in matching warm-up suits; Asian babies sleeping in strollers; boys listening

to iPods, grandmothers in wheelchairs, teens whose boxers and bra straps were showing.

I walked down the terminal and not a single person noticed me. No one asked where I was from, if my hair was real, or if I wanted to get married.

I loved it.

• • •

Arkansas was as hot and as green as Southeast Asia, but it was so clean. I marveled at the wide, shady streets and the newness of the buildings, standing straight and tall, evenly spaced. In the grocery store, overwhelmed by the options of the cereal aisle, I began to feel short of breath. I told Mom I'd wait for her in the car.

The car. Traffic was so orderly and efficient. Cars stayed in their lanes, and never tried to slip through red lights. In my city overseas, it had been all motorbikes and bicycles, all swerving and sneaking, all going at once, without any reference to traffic signals.

Everything here was clean, carpeted, air-conditioned, abundant, quick, impersonal.

I arrived home on the day before my twenty-third birthday, and we went out for Mexican food, of course, because I wanted to eat queso and chips every day for the rest of my life. I slept in the bed with my sister, and the next day Mom made flank steak, creamed spinach, twice-baked potatoes, Sister Schubert's rolls, and strawberry shortcake. My best friend, Anna, who had just finished her first year of med school in Little Rock, came over to eat with us. We were both skinnier than we used to be in college, and I thought maybe this year, our first year of adult life, had been even harder for her than it was for me. I wanted to hold her hand all night.

After dinner Anna and I went downtown to Juanita's, to hear the band Yo La Tengo and eat more tortilla chips, and I felt like myself again. I was speaking regular English, not simplified English with a smattering of words in another language and a healthy dose of hand gestures. I understood all the words that people were speaking to and around me. I didn't have to be on guard. I was talking about indie rock, not boy bands and eighties pop songs. I was wearing my own clothes, not my missionary clothes. The band manager struck up a conversation with Anna and me, brought us frozen margaritas on the house. The boy I went to high school prom with, now a tall, handsome blue-eyed med student, showed up, and we swayed next to each other as we listened to the music.

I was young, and beautiful, and free.

• • •

As the extreme exhaustion of jet lag receded, I had trouble getting comfortable in my sister's big, soft bed. A sleeping bag on our carpeted floor felt more like the thin foam mattress I'd grown used to sleeping on, so I left the bed to her, and began sleeping on the floor.

A package was waiting for me when I arrived home: an affectionate letter from Charley and a smattering of Chinese gifts, including an enormous Chinese sword he thought my brothers would like. I was angry. He wasn't supposed to be doing this anymore. I was angry at myself, too: had I given him the wrong impression, again? We had e-mailed sporadically since we'd broken up in January, and our correspondence had ranged from open to hostile and back again. But it had been weeks since we'd talked at all. Had I led him to believe that getting back together was a possibility?

It was not. I wrote him a letter saying as much, and asking him to stop communicating with me entirely. Apparently there was no way for us to just be friends. I repackaged the gifts and asked my mom to mail them back to him. When he wrote to me again, I didn't respond.

After the initial rush of joy at being home, I felt scattered, at loose ends. My days had no structure, no responsibilities, and I felt the stress of role deprivation: no one here needed me to be a teacher or a Bible study leader. No one needed me to do anything at all. I took my ten-year old brother to the movies, where we watched Hilary Duff trade places with a look-alike rock star in Italy. We ate snow cones and hiked up Pinnacle Mountain with old friends. I tried to schedule my days around the graduate school coursework I needed to do in preparation for the next month's classes on campus, but I had trouble focusing.

Jack e-mailed me, funny, sweet e-mails. He was having a hard time with all the driving. No one walks anywhere! His parents even drove from the parking lot of one big-box store to the parking lot of an adjacent big-box store. He told them he wanted to walk, and he'd meet them there. His younger sister had just gotten married, he said, and he wouldn't be able to come visit me in Arkansas; he didn't have a car. When I went to Chicago in a few weeks, he'd be flying to California to start his master's program in TESOL. He missed rice and tofu, but was happy to be back in the land of sweet tea and porch swings.

One week after I arrived home, I got an e-mail from Veronica. Something had happened. We needed to talk.

17

. . . . .

"The Police Were Following Him"

I had often felt that God had hid his face from me, that his loving kindness had completely withdrawn.

Lillias Underwood, missionary to Korea

I hugged my knees to my chest, curling up in the office chair in front of our family desktop computer, Veronica's voice tripping through the speakers on either side of me. The webcams weren't working, but we were voice-chatting through Yahoo's instant messenger, using new IDs, hoping that no one else was listening in to our conversation.

The girls had gone to a friend's home to meet Philip for Bible study. Like a circuit preacher, he'd taken the train south from the capital to meet them. He hadn't known that the police were following him.

The Bible study never happened. When Philip inadvertently led police to the house, Veronica, Sarah, and Cecilia were arrested and taken to the police station for questioning.

Veronica didn't give me many details. All three girls were interrogated together, and threatened. "If you ever meet together to study the Bible or talk about religion again, you will be expelled from university," the police told them. "And if you are expelled, you will never be able to get a job. You

won't be able to support your parents, and you'll bring shame on your family. Maybe your parents will lose their jobs. Maybe your younger siblings won't be able to find work, either," they said suggestively.

The girls hadn't said much to the police. They played dumb. I felt shell-shocked, but hoped it would all blow over. I wished my friend had never introduced the girls to Philip, as I remembered the questionable things he'd taught them on the retreat and wondered if he was a political activist as well as a Christian. Politics and religion were connected in complicated ways throughout the country, and as a result, the government acted as if anyone associated with Christianity was also a political rebel.

But the questions were far from over. A few days later, police brought the girls in again, one by one. As Veronica arrived, she saw Sarah leaving, but Sarah wouldn't make eye contact. This time, the police seemed to know more as they questioned Veronica. "Who gave you your Bible? It was your foreign teacher, wasn't it?"

The police went to their houses, confiscated their native-language Bibles and the blank journals I'd given them before leaving. Police took the two English devotionals Veronica had, but they left her English Bible and some worship CDs. They told her that I was the enemy. Actually, she wouldn't tell me exactly what they said about me, just that they told her lies about me.

Veronica was scared, relaying the accusations the police had made, the way she'd argued back, the ways she'd given in. She was stubborn, but I could tell seeds of doubt had been planted. She didn't trust her friends anymore, because one of them must have confessed to the police and told them all about me and our Bible studies. I think Veronica must have wondered about me, too—was I a secret spy from America, trying to infiltrate her country and destroy her people's culture?

But most of all, she wondered about God. Was God not strong enough to save her? Did God love Americans more than her people? And if that wasn't true, why was she being persecuted while I wasn't?

After an hour of chatting, we signed off. Details had been hard to pin down as language and fear obstructed our communication, and I anxiously gave too many pat, right-Bible-answers without listening closely enough to her heart. I slid from my chair to the cool wood floor of my family's living room. It was eight in the morning and the sun was already high and hot outside. Most of my family was still asleep upstairs, but I could hear mom washing dishes in the kitchen. I lay flat on my back on the floor, wrung out, tears leaking from my eyes. I lay there and just prayed and prayed and prayed, all my angry words rushing up toward the ceiling.

Why had God rewarded Veronica's faith and passion with this? Why had God allowed our baby church to be destroyed before it even had a chance to begin? Where was God now?

I went back up to my bedroom, opening my Bible to 1 Peter. I read the entire book over and over and over, trying to believe it for Veronica.

In all this you greatly rejoice, though now for a little while you may have had to suffer grief in all kinds of trials. . . . Who is going to harm you if you are eager to do good? But even if you should suffer for what is right, you are blessed. "Do not fear their threats; do not be frightened."

(1:6, 3:13–14)

18

· · · · ·

Instant Messages

onversation with Veronica, July 9, three weeks after our last chat. Messages have been edited for clarity, though I haven't edited out the informal and sometimes confusing nature of second-language internet chatting. I have removed some of our coding, though—when we chatted, we used abbreviations for names, religious vocabulary, and the police.

Veronica: Do you think voice chat is safe?

Amy: Do you feel safe in that internet café?

Veronica: Yes, I'm sure this place is safe.

Amy: Ok.

Veronica: I'm just afraid that this is secretly heard. Do you think they can do that?

Amy: I don't know . . . it is possible, but i don't know if it is very likely.

Veronica: No one knows this ID

Veronica: As you know, from the beginning, the police were after Philip, but since Sarah told about us, now they want to get you and me.

Amy: Right.

Veronica: They even took the notebooks you gave us to write prayers in

Veronica: They threatened everyone but me. They think I'm too deep in that and I'm a true christian

Veronica: They flattered me so that I would tell about you more and more but they didn't know cause I wanted to let them dream on

Veronica: They imagined too much but they can't find evidence

Veronica: I want you to know some important thing.

Amy: Ok.

Veronica: They said to me: "When she comes back, pretend nothing happened."

Amy: They want to use you to try to catch me doing something wrong?

Veronica: Yeah.

Veronica: They taught me about Protestants in other parts of the country doing some bad things, and they said that some Americans want to influence our country

Amy: Do you think they told you the truth?

Veronica: These days, I'm trying to study laws about religion to protect us.

Veronica: I'm keeping some documents about that.

Amy: Good. In fact, I just heard from one friend of mine in the capital. He said that you have broken no laws and that it is not possible for them to stop you from going back to university.

Veronica: About the girls.

Amy: Yes?

Veronica: I haven't met them since then. Sarah is totally absent, only Cecilia understands this problem.

Amy: You must feel very lonely.

Veronica: Yes. Sometimes I cry so much and feel desperate. But it's lucky I still have English Bible.

Veronica: And I'm afraid the others are tempted by the police.

Veronica:	Even me, I was a coward, when the police called my dad and me to the station, they asked me "Do you follow religion," again, and i said "no" because my parents told me to.
Veronica:	But now, studying the law, I have proved that it's my right to follow any religion
Amy:	Even Peter said that he didn't know Jesus, on the night Jesus died. God still used him to build the church.
Amy:	All of us make mistakes and all of us are influenced by our fear. The Father knows and understands and forgives. We must ask the Father for the other girls that they will remember the truth and follow it again one day
Veronica:	Yeah.
Veronica:	By the way, I should confess one thing.
Amy:	Ok.
Veronica:	I need a long time to build my faith in people.
Veronica:	Until that time, I don't want to tell anyone about the Bible.
Veronica:	Really I'm hurt.
Amy:	I can understand that.
Veronica:	Philip is so mature and consistent, I can't be like him.
Amy:	You are facing a strong trial and you have been hurt by your closest friends.
Veronica:	Yes.
Veronica:	Sometimes I try to forgive Sarah, but sometimes, it's mission impossible
Amy:	I know.
Amy:	This is something that will take time.
Veronica:	If the police call me again, I will continue to let them dream on
Veronica:	Never do they find anything from me
Amy:	and it is ok to be very careful about who you tell about the Bible
Veronica:	yes
Amy:	Do you still love the father?

Veronica:	yes
Veronica:	I love Him and I must confess that I wonder about his plan
Amy:	I must confess that I also wonder about his plan—I ask him many times why he is allowing this to happen to you.
Veronica:	I really had some doubt on his Power
Veronica:	However, i know one thing:
Veronica:	No one can snatch me (John 10:29)
Veronica:	and when he gave me Holy Spirit, he never lets me away from him
Amy:	That is true!
Veronica:	It's an identity (the lesson we studied together)
Amy:	I remember
Amy:	He will never let you go
Amy:	and even when we doubt his power or don't understand his plan, he still loves us
	. . .
Amy:	can i give your telephone number to my friend in the capital? He has had some experience with these things
Amy:	and he would like to encourage you
Veronica:	Yes
Veronica:	I'm happy
Veronica:	Actually we shouldn't, cause maybe the police are listening to my telephone calls
Amy:	Ok
Veronica:	I forgot one thing
Veronica:	The police asked me for your tel number and address in America and your email address
Veronica:	They got your email address
Amy:	Ok
Amy:	I don't think that they can access my email
Veronica:	I don't know what they will do with the Bibles you gave us

Amy: Hopefully they will read them and believe them :-)

Veronica: They will accuse you of telling gospel and it influencing our people

Veronica: The necessary thing I should do is that I and the girls must assure that we are volunteers—that we asked to learn the Bible, and that it wasn't your idea.

Veronica: i think the police want to make Sarah and Cecilia say that they are not volunteers so that they are easy to accuse

Veronica: You understand what i mean?

Amy: Veronica, I think it is important that you speak the truth. But I also think it is important that you don't worry about protecting me. Just obey the Father, be truthful, speak with love. And I know that sometimes fear is stronger than the truth, but that is only for a short time. In the end, truth will win.

Veronica: Even one time, they said to me "When you are 18, you seem to be free from your parents but in fact you are still controlled by them. In our country, we say you have freedom about religion, but in fact, you are controlled by us."

Veronica: However, I have enough argument to protest them.

Veronica: But it's bad when I'm alone, and they want to accuse me of not loving my country

Veronica: It's complicated

Amy: I know that you love your country!

Amy: It is possible to love your country and to love the father, no matter what they say to trick you about that

Veronica: I always wonder why our father hasn't chosen my people obviously, so that we are not persecuted

Amy: All over the world, in many countries, even from the beginning, people who love the father have faced persecution

Amy: even today in many many countries

Veronica: Will you come back?

Amy: I will come back in early September, if the Father allows

Veronica: If you don't come back, the police will think I informed you of everything

Amy: I plan to come back. I was afraid that the police would prevent me from coming back

Veronica: No, I told you the police said "Pretend nothing happened when she comes back"—maybe they want to have a lot of evidence

Amy: Well, then I will be there. And we will have to talk about what to do and how to act

Veronica: Yeah

Veronica: I love you so much, I thought I lost you and I resented everything, really.

Amy: You have not lost me. I love you so much and I am always with you. I and my family and my friends think of you every day.

Veronica: Now, I'm really safe

Veronica: and i can chat anytime

Amy: good

Amy: we must chat again

Veronica: Sometimes, we are too weak, but his power will be proved through that. The existence of christians are to glorify Him, right?

Amy: That's right

Amy: absolutely

Veronica: I think I will forgive Sarah, not cause of my sake, not cause of her sake, I just want to honor him

Amy: That is the best reason to do it

Amy: i'm afraid i must go to my class now

Amy: i am so glad i got to talk to you this morning

Veronica: i can understand

Veronica: me too

Veronica: see ya

Amy: see ya

Veronica: try your best for the MA

Veronica:	;)
Amy:	thanks ;)
Veronica:	i love your family
Veronica:	bye
Amy:	i love your family too
Amy:	talk to you soon

Conversation with Sarah, July 18.

Sarah:	are u here, AMY?
Amy:	hi
Amy:	how are you?
Sarah:	ok
Sarah:	so so
. . .	
Sarah:	will u come back?
Amy:	I don't know what classes I will teach next year, but I will certainly be there
Sarah:	oh
Sarah:	i am very happy
Sarah:	to meet u
Amy:	i am very happy that i will see you again too
Sarah:	i really miss u so much last time
Amy:	even this summer, i have wished that i could be with you
Sarah:	yes
. . .	
Amy:	have you seen Veronica or Cecilia recently?
Sarah:	yes
Sarah:	last week
Sarah:	they are fine
Amy:	that's good

. . .

Sarah: do u often learn or talk the bible with ur friend?

Amy: yes. i often learn the bible and pray with my friends in america. today i will go to church.

Sarah: oh

Sarah: bc today is sunday

Amy: yes

Sarah: and who u go with?

Amy: i will go with my friend, my roommate here. her name is melissa

Amy: and what about you?

Sarah: i'm sorry

Sarah: very long we didn't read the bible

Sarah: when that problem happened to us

Amy: yes

Sarah: are u sad about us?

Amy: of course i am sad. i am very sad that you had trouble

Amy: and i know that you must be afraid now

Sarah: yes

Sarah: i see

Amy: but i wonder if you still believe in that?

Sarah: may be

Sarah: but not much when that problem happened

Sarah: i believed in it

Amy: i hope that one day your faith can grow more. there are many difficult things in this life that test our faith

Sarah: but some people made us not believe much

Sarah: bc they said many things we thought not true

Sarah: we believed in u much more than them

Sarah: but may be we need much more time to believe in God

Amy: i know. and you must remember that the most important thing is not to make me happy. the most important thing is to try to love and know the Father

Sarah: yes i know

Sarah: but i knew and believed the father from u

Amy: i know

Amy: do you think that you can talk to Veronica or Cecilia about these things?

Sarah: yes

Amy: all of you need to be able to trust each other too

Sarah: yes

Sarah: pls ask me any thing u want?

Amy: i don't need to ask you anything

Amy: i just want you to know that i am praying for you

Amy: and that i love you

Sarah: yes

Sarah: thank u so much

Sarah: u pray for me about believing in jesus?

Sarah: i believed in him, I just can't learn the Bible any more because of these problems

Amy: yes, about that. also i pray for your health and for the safety of your family, and for your friendships

. . .

Sarah: may be next time i will talk to u many things about that

Sarah: not now

Amy: yes, i understand

Sarah: do u agree?

Amy: maybe later we can talk about many things

Sarah: yes

Amy: yes, i think it is best to be careful about what we say

Sarah: yes

Sarah: i know

   . . .

Amy: ok. i am very happy that i could talk to you today!

Sarah: i'm too

Sarah: i will pray for u

Amy: and i for you

Sarah: yes

Amy: talk to you soon

Conversation with Cecilia, July 23

Amy: Hello?

Cecilia: Hi

Cecilia: Amy?

Amy: Yes, it's me, Amy

Cecilia: Are you fine?

Amy: Yes, I am fine. How are you and your family?

Cecilia: We are fine. All things are good

Cecilia: It is so long since I've met you online

Amy: I know . . . I have been wondering about you

Amy: But Lisa told me that she chatted with you this week

Cecilia: Yeah, some days ago I met her when she was online

Amy: Have you been having any more troubles like last time I talked to you?

Cecilia: No, now I don't have any trouble about it

Amy: I'm glad to hear that

Cecilia: Yeah but I'm really sad because my feelings for Sarah aren't the same as before

Cecilia: She still thinks that in our eyes she is a good friend like before

Cecilia: I can't be friendly to her like before

Amy:	She told me that she wants to be able to talk to both of you like before.
Amy:	I know that you must feel that you can't trust her, right?
Cecilia:	I think now she knows how we feel
Cecilia:	She made me shocked when I met the policeman. She told him . . .
Amy:	I know
Amy:	But I want to remind you of a story: do you remember the story of Peter?
Amy:	He betrayed his Teacher three times
Amy:	But after that, he realized that he was wrong and he wanted to be forgiven
Cecilia:	I know . . . but sometimes when i think about it I can't stand it
Cecilia:	I often tell Veronica that I haven't any noble feelings
Cecilia:	. . . but in fact that my feeling for Sarah is broken
Amy:	You know that the Father can restore all feelings and all relationships
Amy:	Restore—means fix, heal
Amy:	You need to ask him to help you forgive her
Cecilia:	I know
Amy:	and maybe one day he will give you help
Cecilia:	you know i don't have my Bible anymore
Cecilia:	they took all my things away from me
Amy:	I know, I feel very sorry about that
Cecilia:	he took the photograph of you and me and Sarah
	. . .
Cecilia:	I don't like the way the police talk about you and many things
Amy:	I think he told you many lies
Cecilia:	I must tell you that my belief has decreased. I want to learn about the Bible but only with you and I don't want to have another relation with any others (like Philip)

Cecilia: But Veronica told Philip that we want two more Bibles and he agreed to get them for us

Cecilia: but you know i only want to read it. I don't want to meet together like Philip asked us to do when we were in Nicole's house

Cecilia: And I don't want to meet the police again, and hear them say bad things about my teacher

Amy: You know that I love your people and your country. And you are my friend and student and sister. I would never do anything to hurt you.

Amy: And you must also know that the Father loves you and he loves you even when you have some doubt

Cecilia: I know

Amy: What the Father asks is difficult. He asks you to follow him, and there are many trials. You must consider that before you decide what you will do.

Amy: Step by step

Cecilia: I will try

Cecilia: I understand what you are saying to me now

Amy: You should not follow the Father to make me happy. Only if it is something that in your heart He is calling you to do.

Cecilia: It really comes from my heart, with the thing I think about you and I really want to protect my teacher, my friend and my sister

Amy: I am safe in the father's hand

Amy: and so are you.

Cecilia: Yeah

Amy: I hope that this trial and problem can make you stronger

Cecilia: I think so

Cecilia: I remember some sentence in Corinthians but i can't remember it in English

Amy: It's ok

Amy: When you are weak, then you are strong

. . .

Amy:	Do all of your classmates know about what happened?
Amy:	Do they treat you normally or strange?
Cecilia:	Some of them know cause Sarah told them. Some of them act very guarded and secret now.

Though Veronica and I had been close in her country, we didn't meet online very often. Both of us were concerned about the possibility of the police watching or recording our communications, and I hoped that if we just stayed quiet for the summer, the danger would die down.

She still spent a large amount of time online, though, and made friends with a guy named Josh. He was American, from the South, in his twenties, a Christian. They'd talk for hours about the Bible and God. He was also married—unhappily—to a woman addicted to cocaine.

I was not a fan of Josh. His relationship with Veronica quickly grew emotionally intimate, and seemed highly inappropriate for a married man. I worried that Veronica was falling for him, and that he was using her. But there were so many things going on in Veronica's life that I didn't want to make too big of an issue about this one. She was so lonely that I couldn't argue very compellingly against this one relationship with the only person she felt she could regularly talk to about God.

Anyway, Josh wasn't the only one acting with mixed motivations. He may have been using her for companionship while his marriage was failing, but he was probably also genuinely concerned for her, sincerely praying for her. Veronica might have been flattered by the attention of an American man, but she was also hungry for someone to discuss the Bible with. She was in love with Jesus, but she might also have been figuring out a way to understand who she was in general.

And I—I had wanted to save the world, to have a significant life, to have adventures and freedom and to be one of heaven's heroes. In Veronica I'd found an explanation of who I was: a teacher, a messenger—an identity I could settle happily into.

Maybe we were all using each other to figure out who we were.

Conversation with Veronica, July 26

Amy:	Hello?
Veronica:	Hi Amy
Veronica:	I'm Veronica

Amy: Hi Veronica!

Amy: How are you?

Veronica: I'm doing well, what about you and your family?

Amy: We are all fine, thanks

Veronica: 2 days ago, I met Hannah (a classmate who was present at Nicole's house that day), and she said one policeman called her

Amy: Really?

Veronica: And he said that he would continue to "investigate"

Veronica: He said he was busy for a while, but now he's free, so he will continue to investigate

Amy: Well, I think we can be sure that he will continue to investigate us next year . . . we must be careful

Veronica: I know. We will have nothing to say but our Spirit will speak, lol!

Veronica: I wonder what he has to investigate?

Veronica: There is nothing else

Veronica: We are legitimate. We're not breaking any law.

Veronica: My parents say the law doesn't matter. When the police want it to be black, it's black. When they want it to be white, it's white. They can change white into black.

Amy: Your parents are right. The police will not care about the written laws—they will do what they want to do

Veronica: When you come back, we will still be friendly as the old days. I'm not so worried

Amy: I can't wait until I can see all of you again!

Veronica: I will tell them that if they ask me to ignore my teacher, or if they change my exam results, they are bringing shame on themselves and our people.

Veronica: Everything true is tested. As time goes by, the bible will be the truth of my people too

Amy: You are right

Amy: What do you think about Sarah?

Veronica:	Nothing. I can't be friendly to her as before, but I don't hate her. She acts innocent. I don't know.
Veronica:	I need time to recover. And Cecilia can't stand her.
Amy:	I chatted with her this week, and it seems that she wants to talk to you . . .
Amy:	she apologized to me
Veronica:	I met her too. She just said that Amy says we should believe in God from heart, not because we want her to be happy
Amy:	Well, that is true
Veronica:	I don't trust her anymore. She didn't read the Bible, and I think she doesn't understand.
Veronica:	Nowadays, I'm too afraid to talk to people about God anymore.
Veronica:	I am afraid one of them will be a spy of the police
Amy:	I know
Amy:	and I think it is ok to be very careful.
Veronica:	Do you understand me? I can't trust anybody around me, and I hate feeling this way.
Amy:	I understand. and I hope that in time that doubt will grow smaller and your faith will grow larger. But, I also think that it is good to be careful. There is a time to speak and a time to be silent (ecclesiastes)
Veronica:	Yeah
Veronica:	Josh also encouraged me so much
Veronica:	He thinks I'm lucky cause I could understand what is the true passion that Jesus took
Veronica:	But I was a coward
Amy:	I think you have been very brave
Amy:	You have such great big faith
Amy:	When you read Acts, you can see that they faced many trials. But after those trials, always many more people believed in the message

Veronica:	When they asked me "Do you follow religion?" I said "I don't know what you mean 'follow religion,' but the Bible is a great book."
Amy:	Good
Veronica:	They asked me that question so many times
Amy:	I am so sorry that you have had to face this trial and all of their questions and threats
Veronica:	If they ask me once again, I will say "I'm not a christian cause I'm not worthy. Christians are so good, they are never cowards about money like me." They won't know what to think.
Amy:	silly girl
Veronica:	It's a long time since I last heard your voice, I miss you so much
Amy:	I know. I wish that I had a webcam or a mic here so that I could talk to you
Amy:	What about Nicole? have you talked to her?
Veronica:	I met her but I didn't mention anything, and she showed nothing
Amy:	It is so difficult to know who you can trust!
Amy:	She seemed very sincere before this happened
Veronica:	Yes. I don't know who to trust, but I don't feel hate toward anyone.
Veronica:	if i were "old me," I might beat Sarah, really
Amy:	I am glad that you are the "new" you then!
Amy:	I will continue to ask Father to show you and Cecilia the right time to speak to others, and who to speak to.
Amy:	What about you and Cecilia meeting to discuss the Bible?
Amy:	Are you going to try to do that?
Veronica:	Of course
Veronica:	i connected with Philip
Veronica:	And asked him to give me two Bibles again
Amy:	You did?!

Veronica: yeah. My friend will get them from him and bring them to me.

Amy: Good

Amy: I hope there is no problem

Veronica: I plan to get the old Bibles back from the police, too.

Amy: How?

Veronica: When everything ends, I will call the police and say, "Can you give me the books now? They were special presents, I don't want to lose them."

Amy: I don't know if that is a good idea

Veronica: Maybe I will

Veronica: What about you?

Amy: What about me?

Veronica: Are you worried? When you come back, if there is any trouble, I will do anything to stand for you

Amy: I am not worried

Amy: I will always be safe.

Amy: Sometimes I worry about you, but not about me.

Veronica: Yeah, I feel confident

Amy: and I think that the problem is quiet now. Maybe it will come again and we will face more trials, but we will be strong and we will have the protection of the spirit

Veronica: The police said they just want to "educate" us, but there is not any education in threats!

Amy: True!

[Veronica asked me to bring her the newest Backstreet Boys CD. She asked about my brothers and Charley. We talked about dating customs in her country and mine, and her plans to learn to play guitar.]

Veronica: Afterward, when I graduate, I will wait for Father's plan for me about my mission

Veronica: that if I can be a missionary . . .

Amy: I know

Amy: he will make a way for you

Veronica: I think I will preach gospel more truly than some in my country do

Veronica: they never tell others about his passion and death and resurrection

. . .

Veronica: it's 10.10 pm, do you feel sleepy?

Amy: I didn't know it was so late!

Amy: when do you want to meet again?

. . .

19

. . . . .

Saying Thank You
in the Dark

Surely what we want now is more fire. I do not see much sign of it, the fire
that comes from tribulation and persecution, I mean.

D. M. Thornton: A Study in Missionary Ideals and Methods
by W. H. T. Gairdner

Weeks passed and things seemed to have quieted down for the girls.
I drove to the suburbs of Chicago and unpacked my suitcase into
the plywood dresser of a dorm room, slipping sheets onto a twin bed. I took
long walks with Rebekah around the small town, talking about what had
happened to Veronica.

Everything was so beautiful that it felt unreal. Or something was unreal:
I couldn't decide which it was, the persecuted teenagers in an impoverished
town across the ocean, or this movie set that was life in the Chicago suburbs.
Rebekah and I walked to a candy shop, famous for being the narrowest store
in America, little more than a hallway in a row of downtown boutiques. We
went to Borders and bought books: buy three, get the fourth free. When we
drove through neighborhoods to her aunt's house, all the families were playing

141

in their yards. Moms pushed strollers, dads played catch with tousled little girls, whole families pedaled bikes through wide streets.

The mornings were chilly and grey, and everything was clean and open and smelled like fresh cut grass. Suddenly I understood why America was the promised land: the air smelled green.

I stopped journaling while I was at grad school. I couldn't find my words. I'd open the notebook and make a dot, then another, connect them with a line, shade in patterns of grey and white. I'd close the notebook and go for a run, hoping the intense physicality would clear my mind, help me to pray, find some words to say. I wished for a Catholic church, a daily mass that would provide the words in liturgy for me when I couldn't find them for myself. Instead, I ran to try to reconcile the emotions I felt: anger, confusion, sadness, worry, and over it all, the deepest gratitude.

The words of a poem by W. S. Merwin marched through my mind as I walked from classroom from cafeteria, as I rode the train into the city. Listen, he commanded: we are saying *thank you* in the midst of it all, in the midst of muggings and funerals, corruption and decay, we are saying thank you.

My classmates were people who understood how to say thank you even in the darkness. Adam, Rebekah, Joanna, and the others understood the experiences I'd had. I didn't have to try to explain. I relished their presence, tried to soak up their faith all I could.

• • •

Jack e-mailed me:

I wanted to tell you that I've started seeing someone. We're taking it really slowly, but she's a top-notch girl, he wrote. My heart plummeted into my stomach, or it would have, if it hadn't already taken up residence there for the summer. I was surprised; hurt, even. We'd been e-mailing every week or so, flirtatiously, I thought. The previous week, at lunch, Adam had asked if Jack knew that Charley and I had broken up. "I don't know," I'd answered, wondering: did Adam see the connection that I thought was there? Joanna had laughed at me when I'd mentioned him. I had hoped it all meant something.

Could it be that Jack still didn't know Charley and I had broken up? I wrote back, slipping this line into a friendly, chatty e-mail:

The girl sounds great. It seems your love life has blossomed as mine has fallen to pieces—Charley and I broke up in January.

He e-mailed me twice in the space of twenty-four hours, but I didn't respond again. I tried to flip the switch in my heart from crush to friendship, wondering what exactly that coy impulse—the one that had stopped me from telling him about the breakup earlier—had cost me.

• • •

I tried to feel my feelings, for once, instead of denying them any space. Not just my feelings about Jack, but my feelings about everything that was happening in Southeast Asia while I relaxed in the comfort of a Chicago summer. I prayed that God would help me to be more emotionally open, less prone to trying to keep myself under control by stuffing negative emotions.

Throughout my life, my relationship with God had been largely intellectual, not emotional; when feelings emerged, I had often shut them down. Emotions could not be trusted. Only the Bible could be trusted. Emotions had to be justified.

Now I realized that I couldn't feel God's presence at all. Did I love God? I was devoted to God, determined to serve God. "Love isn't how you feel. It's what you do," Madeleine L'Engle had written, and my actions showed that I loved God. But did I really? I felt no love—no warm, affectionate personal feelings, no longing for God's presence.

Did God love me? I believed so. I assented to that truth, but I didn't feel a thing.

Help me to feel that you love me, I prayed.

• • •

I was sitting behind the dorm one day, reading for class, when the sound of an explosion shattered the stillness of our apple-pie neighborhood. Across the street, screams. A garage opened. I ran in the opposite direction.

Inside the dorm, I banged on doors. "I think there was an explosion across the street—can you call 911?" I asked. Greg got on the phone and Bethany hurried next door to get Ginger, a trained nurse. I waited, afraid to cross the street alone.

A girl about my age sat on the driveway, her skin singed black and purple, crying in broken English, "Oh, my God, I am burning alive. . . ."

Her father, shirtless, torso burned red, was crying, mumbling words in some Eastern European language, and her sister, unharmed, couldn't find words in English to explain what had happened.

Ginger told us to pour cold water on the burn victims, and to cut their clothes off. I tried to help, but was so glad when the ambulance arrived. That raw pain, like wordless cries of wounded animals, frightened me. The ambulance took the father and daughter to the hospital; they would live. They would live with scars.

Later that night, I couldn't get the unharmed sister out of my mind. Doubtless she knew some English, like her father and sister did, but in the crisis she could only speak her first language.

I too felt words had been stripped from me that summer. I had thought that I spoke faith as my first language, but as I encountered my first spiritual crisis, I found that I had no words at all. Instead of prayer, or even tears or keening cries, my first language seemed to be silence.

20

. . . . .

Due to
Curriculum Changes

Thus hindered, I could not but realize the hand of God in closing the door I had so much desired to enter.

> Hudson Taylor, writing about his experience
> of being kept from Shantou, and writing many years after the fact

We could not give up—it never came into our minds to do so—but we were sometimes sorely tempted to discouragement.

> Amy Carmichael, *Gold Cord*

You are emotionally distressed," Anna observed as I walked into her apartment near the med school in Little Rock. I'd finished my grad classes and been back in Arkansas for ten days when I got the e-mail from the university overseas.

Due to curriculum changes, it said, *we will not be able to renew your teaching contract for the upcoming year.*

Sixteen days before I planned to board a plane for Southeast Asia, they told me that I couldn't come back. I forwarded the e-mail to Camille and my

teammate Lisa. Camille responded quickly; it was unlikely, she said, that I would be able to teach at any other university in the country, either.

I wasn't ready to tell Veronica yet. First I needed to fall apart and put myself back together.

I suppose when Heaven's Heroes faced setbacks or heartbreaks, they just redoubled their prayers. They snuck past enemy lines. They did the next thing. I tried to pray, and I wanted to sneak past enemy lines, but I couldn't even get back into the country. I had no idea what the next thing would be.

So this was my next thing: I went to a gas station in Anna's neighborhood where no one knew me, and bought a six-pack of hard lemonades and a pack of cigarettes. I took them onto her porch while she studied inside, wanting to do something that was authentic to how I felt. I didn't know how to show God that I was really not okay with being barred from the country except by a small rebellion, so I slowly sipped a single drink and smoked two cigarettes that I had never learned how to properly inhale. With dry eyes and a stilled heart, I wrote in my journal.

This is the information that was gathered later, bit by bit. It hadn't been the university's decision, and it wasn't the local police, either. The order had come from the police in the capital, who told university officials they could not invite me back. Could this mean the police would be watching all the teachers from our organization now?

But local authorities had been keeping an eye on Lisa and me even before the girls were arrested. I heard that Avril and John, two of my favorite first-year students, had been tasked with watching me and reporting back to the police. I wondered if Tina had been, too; I didn't want to know. I didn't want all my best friendships marred in my memory by betrayal.

Rumors swirling around the town, Veronica would tell me, included one that I had been secretly fluent in the local language and a spy for the CIA. I thought back to the final party I'd attended with John and Avril—I'd been able to catch a few words, guess from context some others, and respond appropriately in their language. I'd felt like I was finally beginning to understand a tiny bit of the language. Had they interpreted that as me being "secretly fluent"?

What would I do, now? Over the next week, my options became clear. Camille called me with an update: even if our organization could place me at another university in country, there was a good chance that my passport would be flagged and when I got to customs, the government would refuse to let me enter. I'd likely never be able to get another teaching visa in country.

Still, Camille said, I could wait in America for one semester to see if things cooled down, and try to go back in the spring. Or the organization could free

me from my contract altogether, and I could stay home. I tried to imagine what that would look like: I could live with my parents, I could move to Baltimore with my friend Mollie, I could buy a one-way ticket to France and live at Taizé. I wasn't brave enough for any of those options. Or I was too worried that they were self-indulgent; I still wanted to be serving God, after all. And I wasn't ready to lose everything I'd gained over the previous year—the friendships, the sense of vocation, the grad program, the assurance that I was doing what I was made to do.

Camille called again. "You could go to Cambodia," she said. "Their semester starts a little later, so it's not too late for us to get you in there. And it's an open country—it's not illegal to be a Christian or to evangelize."

The team leader from Cambodia would phone me with details, if I was interested. I waited for his call.

• • •

I decided to fast from noon to noon one day, drinking only water, trying to discern God's plan for me in the next year. When I woke up in the morning, after not eating for eighteen hours, I couldn't get out of bed. As I sat up, my head began to spin, and I nearly blacked out, so I lay down again and waited. Soon I heard my mom putting away clean laundry in the hall closet.

"Mom?" I called, but even my voice was weak. "Mom?"

She poked her head through the door. "Did you call?" she asked.

"I can't get out of bed," I said. Her forehead wrinkled. "I was fasting, and . . . when I try to stand up I black out. I'm supposed to fast until noon. I don't know what to do."

Mom came back a minute later with a bowl of icy cold, cut watermelon. "Watermelon is a perfect food to break a fast with," she told me. "It will rehydrate you, and it is easy to digest on an empty stomach. It's also nutrient-rich. It has all kinds of vitamins and minerals and antioxidants."

My mom was a rule-follower to the core, but here she was telling me to break my fast before the set time.

"I haven't even fasted a whole day," I said, embarrassed. "I used to be able to fast for thirty-six hours."

"You don't really have any extra fat anymore," she observed. "You lost weight overseas. Your body doesn't have any reserves."

All my reserves were empty.

The watermelon tasted like grace, like a promise that I didn't have to be good all on my own. It was the sweetest moment of the summer.

• • •

My parents' church asked me to share for five minutes in the Sunday morning service. I didn't really want to—it was theirs, not mine, and it was the church that had complained about my father-daughter banquet video. I disagreed with the church leadership on a number of issues, and I never felt freedom or grace when I attended with my parents. The church didn't financially support me, though a few families in the congregation did. Despite my reservations, I agreed to share, though—because I loved my parents and because I knew that I had a story to tell. And anyway, this was what missionaries did: whenever we were invited, we shared the stories of God's work in foreign places, we asked for prayer and money, we tried to help people see how big God was.

This time, as I prepared my words, I carefully avoided reading any Scripture or giving any exhortations. They wanted me to share, to tell a personal story, so I would. And this time, hopefully, none of the men would walk out.

That Sunday, I told the congregation what had happened. I'd been sent to a dark, dry, place with no Christian presence, and other missionaries had warned me not to expect anything. It usually took three years in a city before there was any fruit, they'd said. Nonetheless, I'd asked my supporters to pray that by the end of the year, I'd have two or three girls to disciple. One month later, a teacher fell and had to be put on bed rest. I took over her class, and that week, my new student Veronica knocked on my door and asked if I was a Christian.

Through our Bible study over the next few months, Veronica decided to follow Jesus. She was so moved by the gospel that she couldn't stop talking about it. She shared about Jesus with her best friends, and she showed the *Jesus* film to her family, who showed it to their neighbors, who took it to their ancestral village for all the people to see. By the end of the year, three girls had made professions of faith and been baptized by indigenous believers, and three more wanted to join a Bible study. I prepared them to continue studying together while I was gone for the summer.

"One week after I came home for the summer, I got an e-mail," I continued. "Veronica and the others were meeting for Bible study. A Christian from the capital took the train south to meet with them. But he didn't realize that the police were following him, and—"

Out of nowhere, I—stoic, controlled, rational—began weeping. I tried to regain my composure and spoke another few words, but that was as far as I got. I couldn't stop crying, and I didn't know what to do. Would someone come up and finish reading the words I had written to share? But no one

moved. The pastor, still on stage, put his hand woodenly on my shoulder, murmuring something.

I wanted people to come up, to surround me, to lay hands on me and pray. I wanted someone else to cry with me. I wanted them to need to hear the end of the story. No one moved. I closed my notebook and walked off the stage, back to my seat. The pastor said something like, "Clearly a very moving experience of the Lord," and went on with the rest of the service.

As the service ended and everyone began to migrate to the fellowship hall for coffee, no one moved toward me. I felt like they were giving me and all my emotions a wide berth, like I was a wild animal that had accidentally wandered into a human space and everyone was hoping I would just wander out again.

Despite the fact that the church was filled with families who had known me for a decade, only the missions pastor, whom I had never met, called me that week. He left an awkward message on my family's answering machine. Not a single person asked if I was okay—but more significantly to me, not a single person asked to hear the rest of the story, the part I couldn't tell for crying. How could they not want to know?

Maybe to them Veronica was just a disembodied soul I had saved: some foreign heathen I had reached with the gospel, a statistic to brag about, a gold star on a chart. But to me, Veronica was a living, breathing girl: a nineteen-year-old with crooked teeth, long black hair, and a sincere passion for American boy bands. She wasn't a soul I had saved. She was a friend of my heart.

Maybe that conservative, straight-laced Bible church had focused so long on knowing right doctrine that they had forgotten the passion of the Psalms, emotions I was only beginning to understand. Maybe they were just so unaccustomed to public displays of feeling that they had no idea how to respond. Maybe they had never practiced the cry of lament, preferring to focus on easier emotions. Maybe they believed they had nothing to give me. Regardless of the reason, as I walked out of the foyer and into the warm, humid sunshine of an Arkansas summer, I felt emptied out and alone. I had given all I had in that sterile sanctuary, and not a single person responded.

21

• • • • •

Choosing Cambodia

Part of the joy of missionary life is to learn to know (through the most vital of missionary biography) the starry souls who shine now in other skies, and there were some shining like that among us then. But as a company of people set apart for a special purpose, we were, it seemed to me, just dim. There did not appear to be anything burning about us. We were decorously smoldering, we were not vehement flames (were we aflame at all?) and I knew that I burned most dimly of all.

Amy Carmichael, *Gold Cord*

All year I'd been recording my dreams in a journal. That summer, I dreamed about flying.

In the dream, I was living under an oppressive regime and was about to be forced into marriage with a man I didn't love, but I didn't feel worried. Before the wedding, I was assigned to a task with a small group of men and women. We were strapped to a bungee cord anchored to the moon, and then rocketed into space. When the rocket's fuel ran out, we began the free fall back to earth, safe because the bungee cord would catch us before we could crash.

I guess it wasn't actually a dream about flying. It was a dream about being in free fall. Mine had begun.

• • •

151

The day after I fasted, Veronica had e-mailed, telling me that a lot of people in town were saying I was a CIA agent, and that the order to fire me had come from the capital, not the local authorities. Some of the teachers in the capital were under surveillance as well.

Her words confirmed in my mind that I shouldn't try to return to the country. I didn't want to put anyone else in danger. I would either stay home or go to Cambodia.

The team leader from Cambodia, a Khmer-American named Davuth, told me over the phone that they would be glad to have me join them. Their team of eight teachers—six singles ranging in age from early twenties to mid-fifties, and one young married couple—all lived in Phnom Penh and taught at the Royal University of Law and Economics. If I joined them, I'd teach fifteen hours a week from the beginning of October to the first of July.

I e-mailed my prayer supporters about the two options, my heart still so heavy with anguish that I couldn't feel anything at all as I considered the alternatives. Should I just stay home? Or should I go?

Could I summon the energy to invest again? As the summer drew to an end, I fell into depression, staying in bed too long, not eating enough. Without any structure to my days, any work that needed to be done, or any role I was supposed to fulfill, I was aimless and sad. Everyone around me had started school: my sister had flown back to New York, and Anna was busy with med school. Lisa, Jack, Rebekah, Adam, and the other teachers had already flown back to Asia, and I heard little from them. Even Veronica and I decided not to talk as much, to try to protect her safety. Everyone was moving on, their work continuing without me.

I just wasn't sure I could do it all again: new country, new culture, new language, new city, coworkers, students, foods, markets, friends. I'd invested so much last year, and now, while working through the grief of all that I'd lost, I was supposed to invest all over again? I felt like a boyfriend I'd fallen head over heels for had broken up with me, and now a new guy was asking me to fall in love with him. I wasn't sure I was ready for another relationship.

Beyond that, I now knew how hard life overseas could be. What had felt like a grand adventure the previous year felt more realistic, more like a sacrifice now. A year earlier I'd been full of wonder, anticipation, trust, wanderlust—and while I still sensed those things, I also knew what it would actually feel like to be away from my home, family, and western familiarity for a year. I knew how hard it was to learn a language, to begin to read a culture, to constantly adapt, remaining open-minded and cultivating new friendships. A year in a new country is a physically, emotionally, mentally

demanding commitment. Travel had lost some of its mystic appeal for me: life overseas becomes daily life, just like day-in and day-out life anywhere, full of the mundane necessities of sleeping, eating, and working.

Before making any decisions, I did my research about Cambodia. Its people were 95 percent Buddhist. Roughly the size of the state of Oklahoma, it was bordered by Vietnam, Laos, and Thailand. The temperature rarely dropped below 80 degrees. I learned that a thousand years ago, Cambodia had been a powerful, culturally and artistically rich society. And I learned what had happened in the 1970s, when Pol Pot and the Khmer Rouge took over the country, how they had systematically killed all the educated Khmer people—doctors and lawyers and teachers—moving everyone else out of the cities and into the country. Trying to create a truly equal, agrarian society, the Khmer Rouge banned private property, religion, and travel, and shut down schools and hospitals. Men, women, and children worked in the fields in identical black clothing, even identical haircuts.

In less than four years, a quarter of the country's population disappeared—killed by starvation, sickness, or the hands of the Khmer Rouge.

Along with those lives, the Khmer people lost much of their culture, religion, and artistic heritage during Pol Pot's reign. The Khmer generation in college now had grown up with as much influence from the Disney Channel as they had from their ancestors. Since the eighties, aid organizations from around the world had poured money and resources into the country to try to reverse the effects of Pol Pot's genocide. Due to corruption that still existed in the government, most of that aid money stayed in the capital city, Phnom Penh, while the countryside remained underdeveloped and poor. Phnom Penh's newest industries included Gap and Nike factories. The city was cosmopolitan, filled with French, Australian, Indian, and American expats, restaurants, and bookstores.

The first Cambodian church had been planted among rice farmers in the countryside in the mid-1920s, and Bible translation had only been completed in 1999. Since the eighties, missionaries had worked freely in Cambodia. Now, I learned, an indigenous Khmer church, less than a century old, was growing throughout the country.

The English language had been illegal in Cambodia from the time of Pol Pot until 1990, so the country lacked infrastructure for training English teachers at any level. For the previous four years, my organization had been helping develop an English curriculum for the Royal University of Law and Economics. Teaching there, we were able to influence the upper echelons of Cambodian society, investing in future lawyers, politicians, judges, and business people.

There were great needs in Cambodia, to be sure. But could I summon the energy to invest again? I didn't want Cambodia to be my rebound.

And besides, I'd started to remember the things I loved about Little Rock: the way the moon hung yellow over the Arkansas River, then rose white and high, like a baseball headed for the outfield. The first red leaves in the Ozarks, the first nights of cool, dry autumn air. I loved movie theaters and fast food, fall sweaters and road trips. I loved watching my little brother play live music with his band and I began to imagine the things I could do if I stayed home. I could visit my sister in New York, I could be there when my brother ran for student council president, I could bring Anna coffee and scones while she memorized facts about bones and muscles and tissues.

In the days after I e-mailed my supporters about the choice, some of the weight lifted mysteriously from my heart. Lists of pros and cons found a home in the trash can. I knew what I was supposed to do. I could go. I would go.

• • •

As soon as I stepped off the airplane, everything felt right. The concentration of heat, the dusky fish-sauce scented air, the smell of exhaust and cheap cleaners hanging heavy in the humidity. I turned to my traveling partner Kelly and smiled. "It smells like Southeast Asia," I said happily. She grinned. We hoisted heavy backpacks onto our shoulders and headed toward customs.

I'd met Kelly and Patrick in the airport in Los Angeles. Actually, I'd met Kelly before—she had led the informational session about our organization that I'd attended two years earlier. She remembered seeing me there, with Charley, and seemed unsurprised when I told her we were no longer together.

I hoped Kelly might be someone who could understand my grief. I was walking into this new place openly bleeding and clutching my wounds—as soon as my parents had left me at the airport in Little Rock, I'd started sobbing, still unable to process the fact that God had answered all my prayers in the previous year and then ripped that life away from me. I worried that my new teammates would expect me to jump passionately into this new life and service in Cambodia, when I still needed to grieve. I felt defeated and exhausted, inadequate and unprepared for the next year—but I didn't want everyone to see how needy and emotional I was.

Maybe Kelly would understand. She'd had to leave Cambodia due to serious health problems, and after a year in Mongolia, was now able to return. She was a little older than I was, with curly red hair, freckles, and a thick Boston accent. She laughed loudly and relished life. Everything was

"hilarious" or "comical," she agreed with things I said "absolutely," and in surprise or frustration would often exclaim "oyanna!" an expression she'd picked up in Mongolia.

Patrick was a bit quieter, a lawyer in his late thirties with sandy-colored hair and a dachshund named Sam. I felt an immediate kinship with him, like he was the older brother I'd never had. His sister already lived in Cambodia with her husband and three kids—they worked for World Vision. If Kelly and Patrick were any indication, my new team in Cambodia would be good—maybe not all kindred spirits but at least mature adults, seeking to plant their lives across the world.

Davuth met us in the Phnom Penh airport. Patrick would live with Davuth and another single guy, but Kelly and I didn't yet have a place to live. Royal University didn't provide on-campus housing for foreign teachers. Davuth took us to a temporary guesthouse run by a ministry that gave a different trade to girls coming out of prostitution, teaching them to cook, clean, and balance accounts.

We stayed there almost a week while we hunted for apartments. We'd live with Amanda, a sturdy blond from North Carolina with a very conservative background. (At a team meeting later, she'd tell us that her spiritual growth really started at college, which her church thought strange since she had gone to such a "liberal university." When I asked her where she'd studied, she told me she had attended Liberty. My jaw dropped. Jerry Falwell's bastion of conservatism, Liberty? Kelly burst into laughter at the look on my face. "I've never thought of Liberty as a very liberal school," I managed. Amanda shrugged.)

Finally the three of us girls rented the third floor of a building just around a corner and across a street from the guys' house. We would live in what had once been a rooftop balcony. The owners had recently transformed it into an additional floor; the ceiling was thin, and when I turned off the lights I could see still light from outdoors coming in through cracks. We had three bedrooms, each with an individual air-conditioning unit, two bathrooms, a kitchen, a living room, and a balcony. The power went out whenever we ran more than one appliance, a fact I learned during my first shower in the new place: the water, run by an electric pump, turned off three times. Still, the new apartment felt spacious and luxurious, with its cool pink and white tile floors, big windows, and plentiful breezes.

We were within walking distance of both the university and the Russian market, a tented outdoor shopping center selling all kinds of "black market" goods: pirated CDs and DVDs, Nike tennis shoes and Gap T-shirts produced

after hours at the factories, and tourist T-shirts with maps of Cambodia or the Cambodian alphabet printed on them. In the market, we could get lunch or iced coffee or a pedicure, which required only a dollar and a willful ignorance of the possibility of disease being transmitted through a hangnail.

A few weeks in, Kelly and I went shopping together. We stopped for coffee at an outdoor café on our way to buy wicker furniture to furnish our new place. Under a terrace thick with flowering vines, I ordered a rich black coffee and she asked for a mango smoothie.

"You know, I've never bought furniture before," I told her. "Sometimes I wonder what it means that I'm doing all these firsts in a foreign country . . . first job, first apartment, first furniture buying. Will I even know how to be an adult in America?"

"That is funny to think about," she said, smiling. "You didn't buy furniture last year?"

"No, it was all provided for us by the university."

"Does Phnom Penh feel really similar to where you were last year?" Kelly asked.

I'd felt, upon arriving in Cambodia, that I was home again: the smell of fish sauce, the sound of motorbikes honking in the streets, the perspiration dripping down the small of my back.

"At first I thought it was," I said. "Actually, though, I think life here is not going to be anything like my life last year."

I had gone from a small town in an impoverished area to a capital city flush with foreign aid money. From poor students who had never seen a white person before to wealthy students unimpressed by the color of my skin. From a quiet life on a team of two to a very active life on a team of nine; from a studio apartment with space for my introvertedness to a three-bedroom place with two extroverted roommates. From a place without any Christian presence to a place with Christians, ministries, and churches both indigenous and foreign. From one western restaurant that served pizza to restaurants of every kind: Indian, Chinese, Thai, French, Mexican, American, Italian. From shopping for and cooking most of my own meals to having them prepared by a local woman hired to be our house helper.

We lived like expats.

I wasn't sure what to think about it. I certainly wasn't ready to talk to Kelly about it. And I didn't tell her that when I prayed about the coming year, I didn't pray for converts. I didn't ask my supporters to pray that I'd find girls to disciple here. I wasn't sure I'd done more good than harm the year before, and I'd grown afraid of the way God might answer. When I prayed at all, I

mostly just said, "God, help me to believe that you love me, and that you love Veronica." I asked that I would learn to love God more than I loved doing things for God. I asked to feel things.

The churches of my youth had taught me to "guard my heart" and to shut off my emotions, to distrust them. But a book I was reading for grad school quoted Jonathan Edwards, who said that telling people to ignore and guard against their feelings was a work of Satan.

"There is no true religion where there is no religious affection. . . . If the great things of religion are rightly understood, they will affect the heart. . . . This manner of slighting all religious affections is the way exceedingly to harden the hearts of men."

I'd always been so afraid of my feelings. Now, I needed to feel the reality of God's love for me—but all I felt was nothing at all.

22

. . . . .

Why Are We Here?

Cases of incompatibility are of constant occurrence on the mission field. . . .
I suppose we must make allowances for troubles between missionaries by
remembering that the very strength of character which impels them to the
mission work is apt to manifest itself in sharp angles.

Lottie Moon, March 24, 1876

A typical day in Cambodia went like this: I woke early, lifted from my dreams by the sound of water thumping and squealing through the pipes when Kelly showered at five a.m., and I began writing. I brewed a single serving of heady, rich Trung Nguyen coffee in my room every morning while I wrote.

Classes began at eight, and while I could walk to school, I usually didn't. Up and down the street, motorbike drivers were offering their services, calling out: "Moto by lay dee?" I'd hail one and ride to the university. Driving down the muddy road, swerving to avoid potholes and piles of bricks, we passed newly built gated mansions on the left and rows of wooden shacks on the right. I'd walk through a dirt parking lot filled with hundreds of motorbikes to join Davuth and some of the other teachers in the student cafeteria, an outdoor area crowded with plastic tables and stools, and we'd eat salty fried pork on steamed rice for breakfast.

In the classroom, I'd teach reading and writing to college students in uniform, blue or white button-down shirts and navy skirts and pants. The students were like students anywhere—by turns sweet, apathetic, sleepy, and engaged, but none of them seemed interested in Christianity or in me. The beginning of the semester coincided with the last weeks of Cambodia's rainy season. Storms came, sudden and intense, rain pounding on the tin roof so loudly that I had to shout to be heard. When the rain stopped, I could hear dogs barking below, cars splashing and honking through traffic, construction workers in the building across the road, and prayers being sung over loudspeakers at the local *wat* (Buddhist temple).

From my classroom, I could see across the building into Patrick's classroom and watch him pace, pause, and lecture passionately about English for Law to upper-level students. As a real-life American lawyer, he was the rock-star teacher here at the university of Law and Economics.

After class I'd head to our offices on campus to staff the English-language library for a few hours. We had two rooms, with desks, shelves, computers, and air-conditioning, but few students stopped by.

At home for lunch and nap time, I'd eat a bowl of our house helper's tom yum soup, fragrant with tamarind juice, fresh herbs, fish, and shrimp. In the late afternoon, I'd head to a Cambodian language center to meet with my language tutor, stopping off afterward to buy a fresh mango smoothie and read in the shade of a new roadside shop.

Every now and then I'd babysit Patrick's nieces and nephew. I loved being around children, and these were delightful towheads, full of energy for tickle-fights and face-painting. I'd recognized them and their parents, Bill and Heather, as soon as Patrick introduced us. It took me a few minutes to place them, but then I realized that I'd seen their family picture on Camille's re-frigerator the previous year. I adored them instantly, the way they disagreed and still seemed in love, the way they talked about Bob Dylan and economic development all in the same sentence. I wanted to be like them.

On Sundays I'd eat breakfast, sweet pastries and rich coffee, at Java Café. Sometimes teammates would join me, and usually Thomas came, too. Thomas wasn't on our team, but he was from Little Rock, and we'd had friends in common. He was a slender, gentle man with big blue eyes. Before moving to Cambodia to join a Christian order among the poor, Thomas had lived in the same country that I'd been kicked out of. Over cinnamon rolls we'd talk about our mutual friends, our different kinds of work, the story-based discipleship materials he was creating for use among the preliterate in the Cambodian countryside.

After breakfast, we'd moto over to the Church of Christ Our Peace, a small Anglican house of worship with a Malaysian rector and an international congregation. God seemed quiet and distant, and I had grown afraid of asking him for things, so I took refuge in the liturgy, words already formed for me when I had none of my own.

Our team met every Thursday night. For the first few weeks, we used our time together to tell our stories and get to know each other. We'd share prayer requests, and talk about our classes or how to organize the English library.

As the semester progressed, though, team meetings became tense, charged with emotion. It turned out that we did not all agree on the right way to live and work in Phnom Penh. Kelly, Patrick, and I, as the new team members, were still just trying to outfit our rooms with furniture and learn enough language to barter in the market, but the rest of our teammates were bubbling over with mission-minded plans.

The young married couple, Chuck and Meghann, wanted to focus on church planting. They had a book for us to read about making cell groups that would grow and divide into more cell groups, multiplying Christians across the city. Chuck asked us what we thought our goals should be: how many students would we convert, how many cell groups could we start?

"I like your idea," I said hesitantly, "but I don't like trying to make a numbered goal. Shouldn't growth be a little more organic than that?"

What Amanda really wanted was to create an after-school club where students could hang out, play games, and do Bible studies. She also wanted to feed the street children who came around begging every day, and to create opportunities for our students to volunteer at local orphanages.

Leslie, the oldest and most experienced team member, spent much of her free time with friends she had made in the villages. She was teaching them how to budget, how to spot a loan shark, and how to get out of debt, which was nearly impossible to do with factory jobs that didn't pay living wages.

But Davuth, the young Khmer-American, was our leader, and the responsibility of leading a diverse, multi-ethnic team weighed heavily on him.

"We have to focus on the university," he said with finality. "We are here to teach excellently, to witness to our students, and we need to be pouring our energy out on campus, in programs for the students or our colleagues on the faculty. You can do some of those other things, but the school and the students have to come first."

Instead of feeling heard and respected, Chuck (and many of us) felt steamrolled and stymied by Davuth's pronouncement that night.

Instead of supporting our stated leader, when we bumped into each other at the library or met for coffee over the next few weeks, we grumbled to each other about his decision. Team meetings grew quieter, and everyone was more guarded.

Though I didn't like Davuth's decision, after processing it with various members of the team at different times, I found myself in reluctant agreement with it. Contractually, and according to the goals of our organization, we were there to teach, not to plant churches, feed street kids, or conduct lessons in finance in the villages. A focus on teaching made perfect sense for an organization that worked in closed countries, where missionaries were forbidden but Christian English teachers were welcomed.

But Cambodia wasn't a closed country. In Cambodia, we didn't need to teach English in order to be there. Our organization stayed in the country because the government was not strong or stable, and it seemed likely that the country would soon close again to missionaries. In the meantime, though, we spent hours preparing lesson plans, teaching, and grading for students who were among the wealthiest and most privileged citizens of the country. And they weren't showing much interest in us or our religion.

Why, then, come as teachers at all? Wouldn't it be better to come as church planters, or to rescue trafficked girls, or to start a restaurant that trained and employed street children? Surely there were greater needs than English lessons from native speakers.

My friend Thomas, for instance, worked for a group that was committed to living simply among the poor. He built relationships with the most despised members of this society, Vietnamese refugees, and tried to incarnate Jesus in a way that made sense to them in their context.

That kind of life seemed right to me, like the right way to be a missionary.

But I was a foreign English teacher. So I spent my spare time at Java Café and the Russian market, creating a happy, comfortable life, empty of belief, prayer, focus, desire, or love. I sent e-mails on my laptop to people who didn't respond, and I felt myself floating farther and farther away from what I had been, from the people I had known.

Interlude

Google "father of American missions" and the first results that come up point unequivocally to "Adoniram Judson." Judson graduated as valedictorian of his class at Brown in 1807. After graduation, he and a few friends formed the Society of the Brethren, a secret missionary club for college-educated white guys who dreamed of taking the gospel to foreign lands.

Okay, I sounded dismissive there, with my "secret missionary club" for "white guys." And maybe that's unwarranted. After all, these men (and their wives, though they weren't included in the club) did amazing things. Their group formed at a time when the very idea of foreign missions was up for debate. "If God wants to save the heathen," one Baptist pastor told the first British missionary, William Carey, around that time, "he will do it without your help or mine!" Judson and his friends overcame ideological opposition and created the first American mission organizations. Judson went to Burma with the goal of translating the Scriptures and planting a church of at least a hundred people before his death. When he died, he left a Bible, a Burmese-English dictionary, a hundred churches, and over eight thousand believers.

But even if we agree that they did some great things, it's worth considering how the historical moment in which those first mission boards were formed shaped them—and how that has shaped our idea of what missions should look like even today. The clergy who supported Judson's Society of the Brethren determined that to succeed, they would have to form a foreign missionary organization. That's how the American Board of Commissioners for Foreign Mission was born, under the umbrella of the Congregationalist church. Soon after, Judson

parted ways with the Congregationalist church over the issue of infant baptism, and that's how the first Baptist missionary organization was formed.

America had just experienced the convulsions of the industrial revolution and a surge in capitalism, and among the elite, forming corporations was all the rage. The newly formed mission boards followed suit. A new industry—missions—in a foreign land would require, in their minds, investors, boards of directors, executive officers, employees, recruiters, and accountants. That was just how things were done, at least according to Dr. Manasseh Cutler, the moderator of the assembly of Congregational churches. (He's most famous for "buying" a large part of what would become the state of Ohio, displacing thousands of Native Americans, and for bribing congressmen to ensure the smooth passage of the Northwest Ordinance, which would lead to statehood for Ohio, Indiana, Illinois, Michigan, and Wisconsin.)

The first two treasurers of the mission board were known as "shrewd Yankee Christian businessmen," and they needed to be: to send the first missionaries to Asia would require raising $6,000 for each one—roughly $168,000 in today's dollars.

But what if the first missionaries hadn't been sent by an organization which patterned itself after the major commercial enterprises of the day? A less-corporatized alternative might have found more imaginative ways of getting overseas. Maybe Judson and the others could have worked their way overseas, finding "tentmaking" jobs like the apostle Paul, combining financial gifts with some paid employment. Perhaps they could have retained some freedom to determine policy, and been able to remain together even after shifting on a theological point such as method of baptism.

The truth is, the first missionary sent from America was not sent by an organization. The first missionary who went out from America to preach the gospel in a foreign land was not Adoniram Judson. He is remembered that way because he knew the right people—his white, wealthy, well-educated colleagues—the people who had the power to tell the stories, to write the history. But he wasn't actually the first.

George Leile was born a slave in Virginia in 1750. His master freed him at the start of the Revolutionary War, and he became ordained, preaching all around South Carolina and Georgia. He won to faith some of the early patriarchs of black American Christianity, including Andrew Bryan, who led the First African Baptist Church in Savannah, and David George, who went on to found Baptist churches in Nova Scotia and Sierra Leone.

Leile and his wife, Hannah, set their sights on Jamaica. Lacking networks of wealthy friends to fund their missionary endeavor, they indentured themselves

to obtain passage on a ship to Kingston in 1782. There George worked for two years to pay off his debt, and then started a church. The Leiles had tasted oppression, and they were eager for slaves in Jamaica to experience the same liberation, both spiritual and physical, that they had known.

The Leiles labored in Jamaica for over twenty years. With few outside donors, George remained bi-vocational. Without any formal education, he taught himself to read and to preach, and became such an effective evangelist that after seven years, he had converted more than five hundred slaves to Christianity. Over the next five decades, that number grew to twenty thousand, and in 1838, when slavery was abolished in Jamaica, the change was due in large part to Leile's influence in the country.

What if, all this time, American missions had been patterned after the Leiles' example rather than after Judson's?

Highly structured mission organizations have flourished at some points in our nation's history, and they certainly have advantages. But the disadvantages are clear. The organizational overhead costs (for administrative support, communication with supporters, tech support, and member care, for example) can run as high as 14 percent of money raised for missions. And organizations that require missionaries to do their own fundraising end up sending mainly people who come out of wealthy communities, leaving less-affluent Christians (or those without generous and wealthy friends) unable to participate in the work of international missions. The missionary vocation becomes one available only to the privileged in society.

The way we evaluate our "success" as missionaries in the corporation model can be highly consumeristic. The gospel is a product we sell, and we chart our sales effectiveness and use it to ask donors for more support. But if we believe growth in numbers is the sole measure of our health, we have lost our way: humans were not created to be efficient organisms, and God has always been more interested in our proximity than in our production.

As the aftershocks of economic depression have rumbled through the American church in recent years, leaders have begun to realize that even for the middle class, our bulky, expensive models for mission are failing. In 2015, the Southern Baptist Convention's International Mission Board (founded in 1845) announced a deficit of $21 million. They had overspent by $210 million since 2009, draining their reserves, and would have to cut between 600 and 800 staff members.

The IMB is not alone. As many mission boards face these kinds of financial setbacks, they have a chance to embrace the example of George Leile, exercising a prophetic, missionary-minded imagination. What if we had more

bi-vocational missionaries? What if our boards were more diverse, staffed by people who understood the local situation on the ground rather than by church leaders thousands of miles away? What if peripheral theological debates didn't have to divide us? What if we functioned as a spiritual body rather than as a financial corporation? What if we could cut costs by creating more local partnerships? What if we could empower those on the margins to be missionaries by creating lighter, more flexible structures?

What if now is the time to lose the clunky armor and instead pick up five small, smooth stones, recognizing that God's way has never been the way of the empire or the corporation, recognizing that God's way has always been different from the ways the world says are best?

23

• • • • •

The Spirit of Christmas
Past, and Other Ghosts

I asked him what all this fear meant. He said the Ainos' ancestors' spirits frequently go into a snake and the sight of a snake is like the sight of a ghost. This reminds me that one of the questions last Sunday evening was, did I believe in ghosts? Would I visit a ghost-stricken place? "Most gladly," I replied, "at any time of day or night."

W. Dening, "A Visit to the Ainos," in *The Church Missionary Intelligencer*

One morning in class, my students were abuzz with news that one of their friends had been in a motorbike accident the night before. She'd crashed because she hadn't had her motorbike headlights on. "Why not?" I asked.

"Spirits are drawn to light," one girl explained. "At night, if you drive with your headlights on, you'll attract the attention of evil spirits."

Every part of the Khmer life was spiritual. I'd read that Cambodia was a Buddhist country, but it wasn't Buddhist in the way that Americans who do yoga and eat vegan are Buddhist. It wasn't about Enlightenment and Nirvana, and it wasn't atheistic. This Buddhism was ancient folk religion, belief in local spirits who must be appeased, with even a little Hinduism thrown in for good measure.

In October, we celebrated Pchum Ben, an annual festival of remembrance. School was canceled, and students traveled to their hometowns to pay respect to their ancestors. In some places, students took gifts of food to the local wats, and the monks accepted the gifts on behalf of those ancestors. In other places, families threw balls of rice into the fields for their ancestors' spirits to find.

In Cambodia, the past was never really past: whether you believed your ancestors had been reincarnated or were in hell, purgatory, or heaven (and people believed all of those things), at Pchum Ben they were present again, and able to torment or to bless.

Kelly, Patrick, Davuth and I visited a wat on Pchum Ben to observe the traditions that our students practiced. We saw families arriving by bus or car, crammed into the open back of a truck or seated four people to a motorbike, carrying elaborate baskets of food. As I watched them light incense, kneeling in long rows on woven mats on the temple floor and praying that their ancestors would be appeased, I didn't feel the darkness that many Christians have said they felt in such places. The holiday didn't feel spiritual to me. It seemed cultural, the way it feels to go to a church on Easter Sunday and see people who haven't been there all year, dressed in their finest, sitting awkwardly in the pews. It felt like a tradition, a ritual, a fun family outing, a holiday.

I didn't sense an oppressive darkness there, but I'd just had a student who wrecked her motorbike because she feared the spirits. I'd watched farmers who struggled to feed their families make food offerings to spirits. I wanted to learn more, and I started reading.

As I read up on the spiritual beliefs of the Khmer people, it occurred to me that Cambodians would love Charles Dickens's *A Christmas Carol*, with the way that its spirits appeared to Ebenezer Scrooge. I decided to rewrite it for a Cambodian context, and stage a production at the university.

We had forty days from auditions to performance. I was director, wearing long, swishy skirts and carrying stacks of books around campus like Anne of Avonlea. In truth, I felt more like an actor than a director: I loved playing the role of "Director," pretending I had some clue what I was doing. I had no clue—I was bluffing. I just assumed we could make it up as we went along and everything would work out.

I enlisted help from my teammates. Davuth evaluated auditions with me. Patrick helped with rehearsals, and started training a small choir to sing Christmas carols during the play's intermission. Amanda took over the set design and makeup.

After auditions, the cast came over to watch the old, black-and-white version of the movie. We borrowed a projector from the school and watched the film on the wall of the guys' house.

Students came in shyly at first, then started joking.

"Hello, Mr. Cratchit!" I said to the dark-skinned, skinny one with glasses.

"Hello, Director!" he answered. "Where are my wife and children?"

I loved watching them watch the movie. When one of their characters entered for the first time, everyone giggled and the actor would blush with pleasure. When young Scrooge kissed Belle on screen, our Belle, Vansok, a sophomore with crimped hair and a shy, sweet smile, closed her eyes and shook her head.

One freshman who had auditioned couldn't speak or read more than two words of English. Tall and gangly, with pimply skin and a mouth too big for his face, he was smiley and nervous during auditions, but he let the teasing from older students roll right off his back. He was perfect for a role of great mystery and doom—as the Ghost of Christmas Future, he had no lines and a black hood. And it worked! He was great in the part, and the rest of the cast accepted him. He joked along with them, finally gaining confidence.

Two weeks before opening night, I began to get nervous. I started waking myself up in the middle of the night, grinding my teeth. The students didn't have their lines as well-memorized as I would have liked; even when they did, their pronunciation often made the words difficult to understand. Then I realized that our audience—if people even came—might be composed mainly of people who didn't speak English at all!

Davuth and the key actors suggested we make some changes. Most dramas and television shows produced in Southeast Asia were highly interactive. Shows had announcers, hosts who would come on between scenes to recap or explain what had happened.

We chose two of our most popular and beautiful students to host the production. They'd explain the play in Khmer between acts, tell jokes, and award prizes to audience members. We also had them introduce each actor and explain their roles before the play began, so the audience could follow along even if they didn't know English.

I wondered if they would juggle balls, too.

In the week before the performance, tickets sold out. We printed another hundred, and sold them, too. Four hundred people were coming to our show. There were rumors of TV cameras. The students still didn't really know their lines. I grew lightheaded.

But what could I do, five days before the show? I did what I could, and then surrendered control.

• • •

For grad school, I was reading a book about the Holy Spirit. Churches I'd grown up in taught that the miraculous gifts of the Spirit—healing, prophecy, tongues—were poured out only for a time, but had ceased. This book, though, told story after story of miracles on the mission front. Now that I'd met believers from places where the gospel was new, I too believed that miracles still happened—that people had been healed and had spoken in languages not their own, by the power of the Spirit.

But I worried what would happen if I believed it enough to ask for it. What if I asked for the Spirit to fill me? What if I surrendered control? What if I was willing to be used in ways I used to believe weren't possible?

• • •

That week, I posted a picture online, with a caption that referenced one of my favorite Billy Collins poems. An "anonymous" user left a comment quoting a different Billy Collins poem in response. I knew exactly who he was.

Angrily, I e-mailed Charley one line: *I know you commented on my fotolog; please leave me alone.*

It was amazing how his one comment had thrown me into doubt, bringing emotions to the surface that I hadn't even known existed. With a line, he'd made me feel seen and known like no one else could. He understood my references; he understood me. His comment made me realize how much I missed that intimacy. It made me wonder if I'd thrown away my only chance for it.

I thought about something Jesus said:

"When the unclean spirit has gone out of a person, it passes through waterless places seeking rest, but finds none. Then it says, 'I will return to my house from which I came.' And when it comes, it finds the house empty, swept, and put in order. Then it goes and brings with it seven other spirits more evil than itself, and they enter and dwell there, and the last state of that person is worse than the first. So also will it be with this evil generation" (Matthew 12:43–45).

Charley wasn't an evil spirit, but he was someone I had tried to clean out of my heart. The problem was, no one had taken his place. There were empty rooms in my heart that no one knew like he did; when he tried to come back, there was always space for him. Without knocking, he could walk in uninvited, sit down in my wicker chair, take off his shoes, and drink my coffee.

I tried to reach out to other people, those who knew me best, like he did—but they were all in faraway America, living their own lives and not quite able to connect with my experiences.

I needed to fill the empty spaces of my heart by deepening the friendships I had around me, and I tried. I watched romantic comedies with Amanda, started speed-walking around the National Monument for exercise with the ladies on the team. I went out for coffee with Patrick and planned a boat trip with my students.

I wondered if the Holy Spirit could fill emotional spaces left empty by a broken love. I wondered if the Holy Spirit could heal the parts damaged when I'd been ripped away from Veronica, Sarah, and Cecilia, so that I wouldn't be afraid to talk to students about Jesus again. I wondered if I was brave enough to ask for it.

And I wondered about my students, about all the people I'd seen making offerings to their ancestors on Pchum Ben, and the way it had seemed more like empty ritual than bondage to evil spirits.

Could it be their hearts were cleaned out, too, and ready for a different Spirit to take up residence?

• • •

The play was a chaotic, beautiful mess. Some microphones stopped working. Some cues were missed. Some scenes had long moments of silence that weren't supposed to be there.

But the students looked amazing—Amanda's costume and makeup work were great—and some of them gave truly astounding performances. I ran around backstage for two hours trying to keep the actors and singers and crew members and live chickens and chains and ghosts in the right places at the right times.

The audience hooted and hollered, the hosts entertained with charisma, and everybody felt proud.

Their English had improved, relationships had been strengthened, and we'd had good conversations about the cultural meaning of Christmas and the real meaning of Christmas. And at some point in the midst of it, I started to feel like Cambodia could be home.

24

· · · · ·

The Killing Fields

Now let me burn out for God.

Henry Martyn, missionary to India 1806–12

Here's the thing about grief: you think you get past it, like you've turned a corner and reached a plateau, and then out of nowhere it blindsides you again.

This is not a new observation, I know. But I've learned there are things that can make grief even more difficult. Like when you feel guilty for grieving, because it seems like it's been long enough that you shouldn't still be "hung up" on that thing that happened. Or when the loss seems like something too small to warrant such grief. Or when you're a missionary and people think you should be spiritual enough to overcome it. Or when you're a missionary and the other missionaries around you have experienced the same kind of thing, but they speak of it with smiles and unshakable faith, using confident terms like "God's will" and "his sovereignty," affirming "all things working together for good."

Some mornings when I woke up, grief pinned me to the bed, sadness pressing my chest to the mattress, dread for the day weighing me down. What had God done to Veronica, and why?

I woke up sad, I went to bed sad. I cried nearly every day, without understanding why. I waited for the day to end so that I could go to bed. I tried to read my Bible and pray, but couldn't focus and heard little from God. My happiest moments came in the classroom, but even there I felt haunted. I hadn't learned all the students' names yet, and when I saw them I saw the faces I'd left behind: Sopheavy had the eyes of Darcy, Chenda's round face reminded me of my colleague Mrs. Chin, Vola's expressions were just like Minnie's.

We went to the Killing Fields one Saturday. Here, Pol Pot and his soldiers had murdered those they feared—ethnic minorities, Vietnamese and Thai, educated Cambodians, Christians, Buddhist monks, intellectuals, politicians—throwing their bodies into mass graves. Their skulls were piled up behind glass for us to see. Their photographs hung on the walls of the memorial, each person with dark eyes and identical black clothes, identical haircuts. The excavated graves, empty holes cut into the ground, were marked off by ropes.

I compared my grief to the grief of the Cambodian people, like Savun, our colleague who'd lost all his family at once during the genocide. How did these people even manage to go on living after loss like that? Did I have any right to grieve when my experience was so much less traumatic than theirs had been?

But here's another thing about grief: no one else can understand yours. When you have a headache, you're the only one who feels the pain. You might find some words to describe it, but ultimately it's just pain—a feeling—that no one else feels at the moment, or can fully comprehend. Grief is like that; you're alone in it. I couldn't understand theirs, and they couldn't understand mine. It wasn't something to be taken out and examined, compared, contested. Grief is ultimately personal and incommunicable.

And even when it leaves, you still feel guilty, as if your happiness is a betrayal of your loss. If I were happy now, wouldn't that be unfaithfulness to Veronica and all those I'd left?

Some mornings, though, I did wake up happy. The rainy season had passed, and we weren't in the hot season yet. Everything was a rich, leafy green, lush with growth. Patrick called me late one Saturday afternoon.

"I just wanted to see how you were doing," he said. "We haven't hung out in a couple of days. Do you want to go for a walk?"

We took a motorbike taxi to the park by Independence Monument, Patrick behind the taxi driver, and me side-saddled behind Patrick, an arm around his waist for balance. Strolling around the oval-shaped park, we watched Khmer women power-walking, old men doing tai chi, adolescents flirting

awkwardly and taking cell phone pictures of each other. We stopped in an English-language bookstore and browsed, buying novels and pointing out favorites to each other.

"I'm working on plans for my birthday party," Pat told me. (Only his sister and I called him Pat, a nickname he wouldn't tolerate from most people.) "You know I'm turning forty on January 1st?"

"No!" I exclaimed. "You were born on New Year's Day?"

"Yeah," he smiled. "I'm planning a dinner party on the outdoor deck of Friends Restaurant—just our team, and Heather and Bill."

"And Camille?" I asked. My old country director was coming to visit me, Heather, and Bill. She'd known them since they all lived in China a decade earlier.

"Oh, will she still be here then?" Pat asked. "Yes, of course, Camille, too. But anyway, I'm working on a party favor—I want to make a mix CD of songs that have been meaningful to me over my life, and burn copies for everyone. Do you want to help me with it?"

The next day, after church, we went to the Foreign Correspondents Club, a historic three-story restaurant painted peachy-pink. We put our laptops on a heavy wooden table near the balcony, ordered Cokes, and looked out on the row of palm trees edging the Tonle Sap River. Even hooked up to the FCC's Wi-Fi, downloading songs through iTunes was painfully slow. I worked on the design for the CD label, preparing song titles to be printed next to a picture of Patrick's dog Sam.

I'd never heard most of the songs on his list—proof that we were from different generations—but I liked them, especially the mellow James Taylor vocals and the melancholy Bruce Cockburn lyrics. Listening to David Wilcox sing "How Did You Find Me Here," I realized again that I was sitting with a kindred soul. Patrick had known grief and loneliness too, and it had hit him the same way it had hit me. Sometimes I had the sensation that I was about to disappear, but Patrick made me feel like maybe I'd be found before that happened.

• • •

Camille arrived. She brought me a handwritten letter from Veronica, full of Bible verses and spiritual questions and longing, but few details about what was really happening in her life. She brought a bag of clothes I'd left in my old apartment, too. It was like Christmas. Actually, it was three days after Christmas, a Christmas that had seemed all upside down. I'd played

only holiday songs with reggae beats, and my teammates had given me a Cambodian Barbie doll in traditional dress. But with Camille's arrival and Patrick's impending birthday party, I was content.

On New Year's Eve, we dressed up for Patrick's birthday. I wore hot pink linen, a dress I'd designed myself and had one of the seamstresses in the Russian market sew for me. It was like a dream—dusk, twinkle lights, big platters of food passed around one long table on a private patio, all of us laughing and talking over each other. A pop song from the seventies came on the speakers, and Heather stood up and started dancing. "Come on!" she said to Pat, and they pulled us all up to dance in a circle around the table.

Later, we took a riverboat cruise down the Tonle Sap with Bill and Heather and their kids, and visited traditional weavers in villages. I sat next to Camille on the deck, and she caught me up on what had happened since I'd left her country.

Camille brought the kind of companionship I'd been missing—the kind that knows you and sees you, the kind that gets you. I'd missed that, but now, as we talked, it didn't feel like I'd expected it to. It felt like she saw through me, through my pretensions to my fears.

"How are you doing?"

That was all she had to ask, something nobody had really asked me in the previous four months.

"I'm okay," I said. "I did this play at the school, you know, and I'm starting to feel right here." Camille had that counselor's trick of allowing silence to deepen so the other person feels compelled to keep speaking. I continued.

"It's not the same, though. I miss you guys, and . . . I don't know."

She didn't say much, just kept her sharp blue eyes focused on mine.

"Are you really okay? You've been through a lot this semester."

Her one simple question shifted a single stone, just enough to begin the rockslide and move the rubble I'd heaped over the empty places in my heart to try to hide them. After she left, I slipped into the hole again.

● ● ●

While I vacillated between grief and joy, the truth was that I wasn't unhappy in Cambodia. By the end of the semester, as I took stock of the year, I realized that I'd become comfortable in Phnom Penh.

And the comfort and contentment lasted as long as I avoided self-examination. I'd entered Cambodia grieving, but when school started, there was no time or place for my grief. So I'd buried it, and stopped praying, and

stopped hearing God's voice. I'd stopped asking God for things because I stopped believing that God gave good gifts. It felt like the previous year, I'd asked for bread and been given bread; but before I could eat it, it turned to stone in my hands.

I wasn't even sure God existed, or, if he existed, that he was good. Only a week earlier, an earthquake in the Indian Ocean had resulted in the worst tsunami the world had ever known. More than a hundred thousand people in Indonesia were dead, and five hundred thousand were displaced. Where was God in all of that?

I felt like Elijah, who had been zealous for the Lord, and ended up running for his life as a result. *He himself went a day's journey into the wilderness and came and sat down under a broom tree. And he asked that he might die, saying, "It is enough; now, O LORD, take away my life, for I am no better than my fathers." And he lay down and slept under a broom tree.*

My prayers, launched like arrows, hit a blue bowl of sky, splintered, and lay in shards around my feet. I lay down and slept under the broom tree with Elijah.

At church the Sunday after New Year's, our local pastor Wai Mung suggested that maybe our only resolution ought to be, "Have your way in me, Lord."

But God had had his way in me in the last year, and it had left me broken. How could I ask God to do that again?

PART THREE

SURRENDERED

You only need to lose track of who you are, or who you thought you were supposed to be, so that you end up lying flat on the dirt floor basement of your heart. Do this, Jesus says, and you will live.

Barbara Brown Taylor

25

· · · · ·

A Whittled Arrow, Hidden

Today it would appear that we Christians prefer to talk of a measure of commitment, the length to which we are willing to become involved, rather than the depths of God's immeasurable love in which we long to become immersed.

Helen Roseveare, missionary to Congo

Before leaving for grad classes and the conference in Thailand, I took a personal retreat. For one thing, I needed to finish up some assignments. But it was hard to complete homework about the Holy Spirit when I wasn't sure the Holy Spirit was to be trusted.

For another thing, I was desperate to hear God's voice again.

I knelt on a queen-size bed in an air-conditioned hotel room just outside the city, with books and journals spread in a circle around me, trying to make some sense of it all.

I was committed to God. I had already decided that I would serve him: on the mornings when I woke up believing and on the mornings when I woke up and couldn't manage to muster any faith, I would continue serving him.

But commitment was different than surrender. Commitment was about me, what I would do for God. Surrender was about God, what he could do in me.

What if God wanted to do something in me, and did not want to use me at all?

Dr. Helen Roseveare, a medical missionary in Africa for twenty years in the mid-twentieth century, wrote about her recognition that God might choose not to use her, quoting from Isaiah 49:

> Listen to me, you islands;
>   hear this, you distant nations:
> Before I was born the LORD called me;
>   from my mother's womb he has spoken my name.
> He made my mouth like a sharpened sword,
>   in the shadow of his hand he hid me;
> he made me into a polished arrow
>   and concealed me in his quiver.

What if God was whittling me into a polished arrow? What if he was hiding me away, teaching me to be as content in the quiver as I would be when aimed in a stretched bow or flying through the air?

What if God didn't want me to be useful? Could I surrender to that? Was I willing to be useless for God?

I slept and woke, and in the morning I changed into my swimsuit. The outdoor pool at the hotel was empty, and I swam laps until my limbs were shaky. In the hotel room again, I made coffee and ate the banana bread I'd brought with me.

There was something about God's sovereignty that was defeating me. I felt my own purposes and desires and plans had been thwarted by God. But perhaps I had to be defeated—to fail in all the ministry I had hoped and planned to do—before I could recognize my own need to surrender. God does as he pleases, and doesn't have to explain any of it to me.

And he certainly wasn't explaining anything to me. I climbed back into my hotel bed and read C. S. Lewis's *A Grief Observed*, the emotional account he published under a pseudonym after the death of his wife, Joy.

"Meanwhile, where is God? . . . Go to Him when your need is desperate, when all other help is vain, and what do you find? A door slammed in your face, and a sound of bolting and double bolting on the inside. After that, silence. You may as well turn away. The longer you wait, the more emphatic the silence will become. There are no lights in the windows. It might be an

empty house. Was it ever inhabited? It seemed so once. And that seeming was as strong as this. What can this mean? Why is he so present a commander in our time of prosperity and so very absent a help in our time of trouble?"

I wanted to surrender to God, but I didn't hear his voice at all. How could I surrender to an absent, silent Lord?

But maybe I had never known who God was, at all. Maybe my idea of who God is was just a card-house construction, ready to be knocked over at the first hint of adversity. After all, as Lewis wrote, my idea of God was not a divine idea: "It has to be shattered time after time. He shatters it himself. He is the great iconoclast. Could we not almost say that this shattering is one of the marks of his presence? The Incarnation is the supreme example; it leaves all previous ideas of the Messiah in ruins."

When Lewis began to reconstruct his faith, the most he could say was that he sensed a chuckle in the dark.

I asked the chuckle in the dark to help me surrender, then packed my bag and left the hotel.

26

· · · · ·

Falling in Love

Unity, like prayer, like life, may be compared to a musical chord, and I think it must be that our God, who knows beforehand whom he has chosen for us, tempers and tunes us the one to the other long before we meet in the flesh. Constantly we are astonished at the lovely commingling of the very various notes that make up our chord.

Amy Carmichael, *Gold Cord*

The week before I left for Thailand, I got a chatty and friendly e-mail from Jack, apologizing for how long it had been since he'd written, and hoping that we'd get to hang out and catch up at the conference.

I shut my laptop, fuming. Really? He hadn't e-mailed me for three months, with no explanation for the sudden disconnect. Now he thought he could drop me a message and be my best chum again? And wasn't he dating somebody? I e-mailed back petulantly:

Hey Jack,

Yeah, I'm looking forward to Thailand. I'm sure I'll see you there!

Amy

• • •

I arrived in Chiang Mai two days before classes started, and hung out in the YMCA lobby reading books and watching for my friends, jumping up and hugging them hard when they came in: Adam, the dramatic blond; a dancer with a pixie cut named Lissa; soft-spoken Jenny and camp-counselor Hope; finally, my best friend, Rebekah.

Rebekah dropped her bags in her room and came back to the lobby. "Want to go for a walk?" she asked.

We meandered down the dusty road away from the YMCA and toward the Chiang Mai mall. In the food court, we could buy one of the things we'd been missing most—fresh strawberries, washed and sliced and sold by the cupful. Over bites of berries, we caught up, talking about boys, teammates, and students.

"So, are you going to come back next year?" Rebekah asked as we threw our empty cups into the trash can and headed back outside.

"No," I said, "at least not to teach in Cambodia. I think I'm going home."

I hadn't known the answer until she asked, and it surprised me, showing up full-formed like that in my mouth. I wasn't coming back. I loved my life in Phnom Penh, but I wasn't going to come back.

Journaling about it later, I realized that I needed to figure out, before I returned, what exactly I believed about missions. A year and a half overseas had made me wonder if meaningful cross-cultural exchange was even possible, or if it was always too fraught with complexity to be beneficial. I had said no, and they had heard yes. I had said "thank you," and they had heard, "we're not friends." I had begun to learn a few words of their language, and they had heard, "I'm actually a CIA spy."

Sometimes, too, I worried about the power differential between teachers and students. I didn't want to talk about Jesus from a place of authority, or in any way that would be coercive.

I didn't feel called to teach in Cambodia; in fact, maybe I didn't believe in the work we were doing in Phnom Penh. I might have continued to request support to teach English in a closed country, but if I were going to ask people for money to go to an open country like Cambodia I wanted to do something more directly helpful or evangelistic. What seemed most needed in Phnom Penh was either development work, correcting the unjust systems that left so many people in various kinds of bondage, or the work of training and supporting indigenous Christians who went into the countryside as missionaries to their own people. If I ever came back, I'd want to be involved in one of those efforts.

But maybe I could support those kinds of work better by sending money from the States.

I stopped at an Internet café to send some e-mails, while Rebekah went back to the YMCA to unpack. An hour later, at twilight, the streets were quiet as I walked back alone. On either side of me, houses on the residential street were hidden behind gates and flowering vines. Ahead of me, I could see a tall, skinny guy walking in my direction. We were the only two people on the street, and we recognized each other long before we were close enough to speak, leaving us with a long, silent minute of an awkward approach. To make eye contact or not to make eye contact? To shout a greeting or to wait? To speed up or maintain an even pace? To smile or look away?

He smiled widely, and I managed to curve my lips upward. I felt my linen skirt flipping against my knees.

"Hey! How are you? Where are you going?" Jack said.

"Hey. Good, yeah, just checking my e-mail then going back to the Y," I said quickly, without fully stopping in the road. "I'll see you back there," I said, continuing.

My cheeks flushed as I passed him. This was okay. He was still cute. But my crush had been over for months now. I was cool.

I was cool for about a day and a half.

The next morning, at breakfast in the YMCA cafeteria before classes began, Jack brought his tray over to the table where I sat with Lissa, Rebekah, and Adam. He sat down next to me. "So, what are we doing today?" he asked.

"There's a new coffee shop inside the mall—Black Canyon Coffee," Adam offered.

"I have to go to the mall after class to pick up a few things anyway," said Lissa. "Maybe we could meet at the coffee place around four?"

"As long as we don't stay too long—I'm supposed to have dinner with my teammates," Rebekah agreed.

"Sure," I managed. "Sounds fun."

As we finished our scrambled eggs, toast, and fruit, Jack turned to me. "Hey, I brought a couple of mix CDs for you," he said. "I need to go the Internet café to print out the track lists, but I'll try to get them to you tonight."

"Really?" I said. "Wow. Thanks." He had brought me two CDs, and track lists on a thumb drive? Maybe he really had been thinking about me. I wondered.

And so our two weeks of grad school fell into a pattern: every morning at breakfast, Jack would ask what we should do that day. Then the two of us, with our rotating groups of friends, would spend the afternoons or evenings

together. We went to eat Italian food at a restaurant on the river, sitting at long picnic tables with paper lanterns strung above our heads. We sang karaoke—by now we knew the European pop stars that our Asian students loved best, so we sang songs by the boy band Blue and the female duo M2M.

When I skipped breakfast one day, Jack called my room in the afternoon and asked if I wanted to go for a walk. We went to a thrift shop, looking for secondhand shirts, and planned a surprise birthday party for our friend Jenny. At the mall, we ordered an ice cream cake and got her a present.

One night Jack found a film festival at a Thai university. They were show-ing *Metropolis*, a silent German film from the 1920s, on the rooftop. A dozen of us crowded into two tuk-tuks to ride across town, then climbed the stairs to the roof of the college art department. The night was cloudless and cool, the movie quiet and astonishing, but I wasn't sitting next to Jack, so I was distracted. Wishing our shoulders were touching, I suddenly found that I wanted nothing more than to sit beside him every day for the rest of my life, watching classic movies in black and white, finding beautiful and surprising things in foreign places forever.

But he hadn't said anything.

Other people were saying things. They began to use the plural "you" to talk about us, like we were an us. *You like to linger over your meals*, they said when they passed us at Lanna Café.

Adam asked, "Is there something you need to tell me?"

Hope confided, over lunch, "My friend—who has her master's in psy-chology—asked if there was something going on between you and Jack." I told her I wasn't sure if he liked me or was just being his normal kind, generous self. I'd noticed from the first time I met Jack that he was always including those on the outskirts of groups. Maybe that's all that was happening here. Hope didn't agree, citing more of her friend's observations. "She said that she can tell that he's always very aware of what you're doing. And Shannon said you always look happy, like you're in love." Shannon was a second-year teacher working in China. "Shannon doesn't even know about Jack."

That very first night, he'd given me the CDs he'd brought. We were all playing cards in Adam's room, sprawled over the beds and on the floor, snack-ing on a carton of mango slices from the small shop across the street. Adam was teaching me the rules to Hearts when Jack came in.

"I've got your CDs," he said. "Actually, let's put one on. Where's your computer, Adam?" He slipped the first disk into Adam's laptop.

"This song is amazing," Jack told me. "Have you ever heard Joanna Newsom?"

It was one of those moments, like in a movie when the rest of the scene fades away and everything goes quiet except for the one sound that matters. I stopped hearing instructions for Hearts, and heard only Joanna Newsom's weird, creaky, freak-folk voice waver out from the speakers. She played the harp, and sang:

> And some machines are dropped from great heights lovingly
>
> And some great bellies ache with many bumblebees, and they sting
> so terribly

I knew, from that first night, really, that Jack understood. He understood that beauty was strange. He understood that Someone dropped machines from great heights on our dreams, crushing them—and that sometimes, this was love. Jack had made friends with sorrow; he was attentive to the beautiful and terrible things in the world, and he was unafraid. I didn't admit it to myself, but I loved him right away.

● ● ●

On the last night of grad classes, we all watched a movie in my room. Everyone filed out, sleepy, as the movie ended, except Jack. "See you tomorrow?" he asked as he opened the door to leave.

"Yeah, maybe." I was always trying to be the elusive one.

"Maybe?" he asked, and I smiled.

"I would like to see you tomorrow," I amended.

"We've been seeing a lot of each other," he said, closing the door and coming back in, perching lightly on the bed. "I've really enjoyed it. I'd like to keep spending time with you."

It was the moment to awkwardly define our relationship. I admitted that I wanted to get to know him better too, but I was scared. That girl he'd been "sort of" dating at the beginning of the year—hadn't that relationship fizzled out because they hadn't been able to keep up the long-distance communication? Why would it be any different for us?

"This is just different," he said. "I really want to try to make this work. Do you?"

I worried that he was too quiet and private. I worried that we were too alike, both introverts who took forever to open up. I worried that he wouldn't like me once he really got to know me. I worried that he wasn't really interested in me, specifically, but just looking for someone to marry. I worried that he

was suffering from what a friend called "the fencepost syndrome"—the way that, after being in an isolated setting for a long time, away from any romantic prospects, even a fencepost begins to look alluring.

But I knew this time that I wanted to choose courage instead of self-protection, daring instead of doubt. I wanted to give up trying to control or rationalize my feelings, and instead just let them exist.

I wanted to try love.

27

• • • • •

Being the Beloved

God has made me a new man! I have not got to *make* myself a branch, the Lord Jesus tells me I *am* a branch. I am *part of him*, and have just to believe it.

Hudson Taylor, reflecting on John 15:5

At the opening session of the conference, we read Isaiah 42:

Behold my servant, whom I uphold,
    my chosen, in whom my soul delights;
I have put my Spirit upon him;
    he will bring forth justice to the nations.
He will not cry aloud or lift up his voice,
    or make it heard in the street;
a bruised reed he will not break,
    and a faintly burning wick he will not quench;
he will faithfully bring forth justice.
    He will not grow faint or be discouraged
till he has established justice in the earth;
    and the coastlands wait for his law.

As we read the familiar verses aloud, I finally understood where I fit in the picture they painted. I was not the one chosen to bring justice to the

nations. I was not the one for whom the coastlands waited. I was the faintly burning wick.

The fiery passion I'd taken overseas had been nearly extinguished by the realities of cross-cultural work, by God's silence in response to my despair over what had happened to Veronica. I was a faintly burning wick, in a lamp nearly empty of oil, but here was a promise: I would not be extinguished. I held on to that promise.

After the Scripture reading, we sang a hymn, and then the speaker took the stage. He led us to Leviticus 6, a chapter including instructions for the priests who tended fires on the altar where burnt offerings were made to God. After an offering had been reduced to ashes, the priest was to carry the ashes outside the camp—to clean off the altar before the next offering.

"Your lives have been a living sacrifice, burning on the altar to God this year," the speaker said. "We need to take some time to clean out the ashes, to deal with the past—the wounds, the failures, the joys, the successes. We must pause and deal with the past before we move on."

We would take a day of Sabbath rest: no programming, no meetings, nothing but time to mentally and emotionally and spiritually clean out the ashes and rest with God.

I sat on a dark wooden bench in a gazebo, surrounded by yellow chrysanthemums, delicate orchids, and trailing roses, and watched the shadows of the willow trees dance on the green hillside. As I contemplated the ashes of the previous eighteen months, I felt the sad emptiness that Job described so well:

> "How I long for the months gone by,
>   for the days when God watched over me,
> when his lamp shone upon my head
>   and by his light I walked through darkness!"

Job 29:2–3

I, too, mourned the loss of intimacy with God that I had experienced, the loss of spiritual success. Why had God absconded? Like Job, I blamed God and his sovereignty for everything that I'd lost:

> "He throws me into the mud,
>   and I am reduced to dust and ashes.
> I cry out to you, God, but you do not answer;
>   I stand up, but you merely look at me."

Job 30:19–20

When I cleaned out the ashes of my sacrifice, I found that I had nothing but them to offer. Surely God was a consuming fire, and all my virtue had been burned away.

• • •

That evening, we met for music and the Eucharist. As I slipped out of my seat, into the line of people moving toward the front to take the bread and the juice, I felt hollowed out, empty.

I did not feel the thrumming passion I used to experience at conferences like OneDay, where the baseline thumped through my chest.

I was not committing my life afresh to God, or promising to obey him. I was not raising my hand to pledge a year of service overseas.

My eyes were dry—no great emotion fueled my movement toward the table.

And for the first time in my life, I understood what the Eucharist meant.

Eucharist, in the Greek, comes from two words—"good" and "gift." This was the first time that I understood what it meant that the body and blood of Christ were God's good gift to me.

I had known from childhood that God's love was not something I could earn. Since the age of six, I'd known that we are saved by grace, through faith, and this is not of ourselves—it is the gift of God. Not by works, lest any man should boast. And I had believed that.

But I had never felt the reality of it, because I had never been before God with nothing to offer. I had always had my virtue, my obedience, my Bible memorization, my leadership in the youth group, the Bible studies I led, the girls I mentored, the hours I'd spent singing praise songs, the commitment I'd made to serve him overseas.

All I had now was a semester I'd spent avoiding ministry, walking in the dark and listening for God's chuckle. All I had was an unused altar, finally cleaned of the ashes of anger and regret.

Now, I walked toward God with empty hands and heart, and for the first time, as I tore off a too-big chunk of bread and dipped it into the cup of juice, I understood that I didn't deserve it.

And I understood what I had always believed: that God loved me anyway.

God accepted me. It was a message I had heard in churches all my life. But it had usually been followed by something—a *but*, an *and*, a *so*. God loves you, and in response to his great love, you will want to read your Bible more, fast and pray, tell the lost about Jesus. God loves you, so you shouldn't worry, doubt, or fear. God loves you, but he doesn't want you to stay the same.

In the mountains of Chiang Mai, I finally understood, both mentally and emotionally, that the sentence didn't need anything added. God loved me. Full stop.

In high school I might have told you, if you'd asked, that my "life verse" was Luke 12:48: "To whom much has been given, much will be required." I had known God from the cradle. I'd grown up in a happy Christian family and had every material advantage. So much had been given to me, and I was weighted with the responsibility of doing much with it.

When I visited third world countries as a teenager, I recognized that I hadn't just been given the advantage of a happy family and a Christian upbringing, but I'd been given the advantage of being American: I had opportunity and wealth and security. The weight of responsibility shifted subtly into guilt: if I didn't find some way to selflessly give back some of my privilege, how could I live with myself? I had to do big things. I had to make a difference. I had to deserve what I'd been given.

But now I was wondering what "big" even meant. Had Jesus made a distinction between "big" things we could do for God and "small" things we could do for God? Was "making a difference" really something I was called to do—was it even possible? No verse in my New Testament asked me to make a difference. According to Jesus, I wasn't supposed to *try* to be "salt and light" to a desperate world; I already was. It wasn't something to do; it was the very identity I'd been given.

At church a few weeks prior, after the Indonesian tsunami, my Malaysian rector Wai Mung had reminded us that Jesus entered a world that was full of political corruption, social inequalities, unfair taxation, illness, poverty, hunger—and that when he left, thirty-three years later, there was no visible change in any of those areas.

It is easier, Wai Mung had said, to serve Jesus than to follow Jesus. It was easier to commit than to surrender. It was easier to work for him than simply to accept my identity, and to walk in the world as the Beloved of God.

I hadn't been able to understand that I was loved by God until I stopped doing anything for him. I had to stop being "useful" before I could believe that I was loved. That night, I ate the bread and drank the juice, and knew for the first time that regardless of what I had or hadn't done for God, he was delighted with me. I might be a smoldering wick, all but extinguished; even so, I was God's Beloved.

28

. . . . .

Fireflies and Honey

Cross-loving men are needed.

from *Hudson Taylor's Spiritual Secret*

Despite my infatuation with Jack, I filled my journal with the worries I had, too. There was the obvious introversion, the quiet nature that—coupled with my own—might keep us from ever really connecting. I couldn't tell what his great passions in life were, and that made me wonder if he was too passive.

As a teenager, I had been taught that I was supposed to find a "real man"—and that REAL was an acronym. A real man Rejected passivity, Expected the greater reward (you know, the one stored up in heaven), Accepted responsibility, and Led courageously. These sounded to me like things that all humans, not just men, should do. Nonetheless, I had, almost without realizing it, internalized the idea that if I wanted to get married, I had to find a REAL man who was strong enough to lead me.

I had learned, early on, how to quiet myself, to make my strengths less obvious, so that I wouldn't be as intimidating to guys. By the time I graduated from high school, I had stopped answering as many questions in class and started hiding my papers so no one could see the grades. I grew embarrassed

rather than grateful when my accomplishments were announced; I was relieved to be named salutatorian, with my buddy Sean the valedictorian.

It seemed the best way to support a man—to be "a helper," as we were told Eve was created to be, and obviously that meant she was not dominant in any way—was to limit myself, to not take the spotlight away from him, to encourage him to be his best rather than trying to be my best. In college I felt that marriage would be horrible, an endless life of cheerleading for a boy too weak to succeed without my constant encouragement. After all, what kind of man would only be willing to marry a woman who was weaker than he was?

When I tried to imagine this mythical Leader, I could only imagine someone whose abilities surpassed mine in every area of life: whose test scores and grades were higher than mine, who knew more Bible verses than I did, who could best me in theological argument, who was a more dynamic teacher than I was, a more charismatic personality, more disciplined, more likely to be on stage.

Jack was certainly a nice guy, and disarmingly good-looking. But what if I had more drive and ambition than he did? Did that mean I couldn't marry him?

On one of the last nights of conference, we sat in a circle on the floor with Adam, Rebekah, Hope, and Lissa, playing the Dictionary Game. The game is simple enough: one person finds a word in the dictionary that she's reasonably certain no one has ever heard. She pronounces it, spells it, and then everyone makes up a definition for it, writing their definitions on scraps of paper passed to the one holding the dictionary. She then reads all the definitions, false and true, and every player has to guess which is the real one. You win points for guessing correctly, and you also win points for writing definitions that fool other people.

The game had ended with Jack and me squarely tied for first place, Adam muttering (to my delight) that we were clearly a match made in heaven. As we walked out into the cool night air, I felt relieved. Jack could match me in verbal wordplay, at least. (To be honest, that was the only night I matched him—since then, he's beaten me at every single round of Scrabble we've played.)

"I heard there's a coffee shop up the road," Jack said. "Do you want to check it out?" It was much too late for coffee—the stars were out, and they were our only light on the dirt road up the mountain—but of course I said yes, anyway. As we hiked up the incline, I saw a dim light through the thick forest ahead.

It was a Thai place, a wooden platform jutting out on the side of the mountain, a mostly open-air shop, decorated with posters of European pop stars.

No other customers in sight, we took our small, dark coffees out on the deck and sat on the edge, our legs dangling over the precipice. We talked about how hard the last semester had been for both of us. Jack had spent his whole first year in the country in the honeymoon phase of culture shock, blissfully taking in all the new and delightful differences he found—but when he returned, all the newness had worn off. He found himself lonely and unmotivated.

We talked about going back to the States. Neither of us knew what we would do there, though Jack figured he would move to California to finish his master's degree.

"What do you want to get out of life?" I asked. "I mean, when you dream about the future, what do you see?"

We sat side by side, both looking into the dense tangle of forest below us. I was glad we weren't facing each other. I wasn't trying to get him to say that he dreamed of being married, or that he dreamed of being married to me. I just wanted to know him better. But some questions are easier to ask when you don't have to make eye contact.

"I don't know," Jack said. He had never had any strong, specific career ambitions. "But I've always looked forward to the day when I'm a grandfather, and I'm just sitting on the front porch, drinking sweet tea and playing guitar."

Jack had told me about his grandparents, the house they owned on Ed's Lake Road. When he was in college in the mountains of Tennessee, he'd drive an hour to spend weekends with them, helping with odd jobs around their property, suiting up and harvesting honey from their bee hives. To Jack, his grandparents were a picture of how a quiet, simple life could be beautiful. They weren't likely to talk much about their faith, he said, but they lived with such kindness and joy that you didn't need to ask.

So when he said he wanted to be a grandfather, I knew what he was saying: that the things that would make his life meaningful were not great achievements, as some might measure them, but small joys: a happy family, a creaky porch swing, an ice cold drink on a humid summer evening, fireflies and honey.

And suddenly my way of measuring achievement, ambition, and success seemed wrong-headed, maybe even petty. There was another way to understand life: it was not only about accomplishment. It was not only about the things you did: it was about the person that you became.

What I needed was not a Leader; someone stronger than I was in every way, someone competing in the same race that I was, but always just a little bit faster. What I needed was a companion in whom I could see the fruits of the Spirit that I hoped would develop in myself as well.

And Jack was patient. I had never seen him angry. He was kind. In groups, he quietly and consistently looked for the person on the margins, the one who might be feeling left out, and made sure that person was included. His manner was characterized by peace; there was a steadiness and stability to him that reassured me. He was diligent and responsible; he did his grad school work, and he went to class on time. He was humble, never expecting special treatment, wary of too much attention. He took great pleasure in the small beauties of the world: a well-framed photograph, the right word choice in a poem, a clever rhyme in a song lyric, the flavor of mint and cilantro in a noodle dish. He wasn't the kind of leader who grasped for power, who sought out roles of authority and influence: he was the kind of leader people naturally gravitated toward because of the kindness, integrity, and joy that radiated from him.

"God gives gifts to his children, and he knows which gifts will be most pleasing to which children. You are God's perfect gift to me," Jack later wrote in a letter to me.

He was not what I had thought I needed: he didn't have savvier theological arguments, higher test scores, more "spiritual success," or any desire to be the guy on stage. In him there was not an ounce of pretension or hypocrisy. Maybe I hadn't needed a "leader" at all; just someone to walk through life with, enjoying every one of God's good gifts together.

29

•••••

Gethsemane

We must follow in his footprints. The pioneer missionary, in overcoming obstacles and difficulties, has the privilege not only of knowing Christ and the power of his resurrection, but also something of the fellowship of his suffering.

Samuel Zwemer

Conference ended, and we went back to work. Jack came to visit me. We went to the beach with his teammate Greg, ate Indian food, and flipped through racks of pirated CDs in a shop that catered to backpacking American twentysomethings.

Later, I visited him. I hadn't been sure I'd be able to reenter his country, but going to the embassy for a visa, I inadvertently went to the "back door," getting an expedited, under-the-table document. I took a bus to a shuttle to the border, got food poisoning, threw up on the side of the road, and got in yet another vehicle, riding in the open back of a pickup to the next border crossing. But eventually I made it. Jack and I cooked together and watched Hitchcock films and kissed in a hammock on the porch.

We'd met each other's students. We'd made mistakes; we'd forgiven each other. We slowed down; we sped up. I put on Dr Pepper lip balm for our Yahoo video chats once a week; Jack proved he could handle long distance, e-mailing me almost every day.

I was in love but, shockingly, romantic happiness did not cause all the other complications of my life to disappear. My relationship with God remained mysterious and confusing.

It was true that God's silence had ended; I was praying now, and hearing God answer my prayers. One afternoon, stressed about the future and career decisions, I went for a long walk downtown, along the Tonle Sap River. I was in a neighborhood I rarely visited, but I wished I could find someone to counsel me, to speak into my distress. I asked God to let me run into Heather. Minutes later, I saw her walking toward me.

When I had doubts about Jack, I prayed about them, and his next e-mails would often directly address the questions I'd laid before God.

But these answers to prayer, encouraging as they were, didn't help me understand why God had absconded when Veronica was arrested. I wanted God to explain himself! I wanted God to prove to me that he cared about Veronica and was with her, as he was with me.

As Easter Sunday approached, I found myself lingering in the shadows of the Garden of Gethsemane, thinking about God's silence in the face of Veronica's suffering.

A good friend had once confessed to me that she found herself praying a prayer for me that made her bite her tongue. She'd starting praying from Philippians 3: "God, I ask that Amy would know Christ, and the power of his resurrection, and the fellowship of sharing—" and then she stopped, wondering if she could really ask for another person to know the fellowship of sharing in Christ's sufferings. Should she? Did she have the slightest idea of what she might be requesting with such a prayer?

Yet Paul clearly desired it for himself—he wanted to "know Christ, and the power of his resurrection and the fellowship of sharing in his sufferings, becoming like him in his death, and so, somehow, to attain to the resurrection of the dead" (Philippians 3:10).

What does it mean to share in Christ's sufferings—to become like him "in his death"?

A year before, I hadn't been thinking about Christ's suffering so much as his glory. A year before, you would have found me outside the empty tomb, or running to find the disciples, or waiting expectantly in the upper room. You would have found me exulting in the resurrection, and the new life I'd seen in Veronica, Sarah, and Cecilia.

But this Easter, I was lingering over Christ's passion, feeling the emotions that T. S. Eliot captures so well:

> After the torchlight red on sweaty faces
>
> After the frosty silence in the gardens
>
> After the agony in stony places
>
> The shouting and the crying
>
> Prison and palace and reverberation
>
> Of thunder of spring over distant mountains
>
> He who was living is now dead
>
> We who were living are now dying
>
> With a little patience.

I stayed in this scene not because I couldn't find faith to believe in the next, but because the passion of Christ had never meant as much to me. I thought back over the previous year.

I'd prayed, the summer before in Chicago, that God would teach me to be emotionally open to him. I loved God with my mind and strength and soul, but I didn't love him with my heart. I didn't know how. I asked God to bring me into a real relationship with him—to give me a heart that loved him.

But there was no change in my heart, and as summer bumped up against fall, I found out that I couldn't return to Veronica and her university. All my plans for the year were thwarted and my heart was broken, not only because I couldn't return but also because those sweet girls had lost their Bibles, their faith in each other, and the uncomplicated joy of salvation. They faced opposition before they had even really begun. In confusion, I'd taken what felt like the only option open to me, and moved to Cambodia.

I had prayed, and I tried to see purpose. I had prayed and asked God to open my heart to him. I asked him to teach me to surrender completely to him and to his plan. But I doubted everything about the work I was supposed to be doing in Cambodia, and walked through my days empty and faithless. I asked for answers.

I had heard no answers. My heart remained hard, and my doubts only multiplied. My prayers, more and more rarely offered, never pierced the blue-bowl ceiling of the sky, just littering the field around me, abandoned shafts and feathers.

God was silent.

From the Garden of Gethsemane to the cross, God was also silent. While his Son (his beloved Son, in whom he was well-pleased) prayed, sweating

blood, asking for the cup to be removed, God was silent. When his Son cried in agony, "My God, my God, why have you forsaken me?" God was silent.

German Protestant theologian Jürgen Moltmann writes:

> Christ's true passion begins with the prayer in Gethsemane which was not heard, which was rejected through the divine silence. . . . This godforsakenness is the cup which he is not spared.

The scandal and the glory of our faith is that it hinges on this most awful moment in history, when God forsook God; when the deepest cry of anguish the earth has heard was met with silence. Our God, alone of all the gods, experienced the full extent of human suffering.

Moltmann continues:

> A real answer to this question ["My God, my God, why have you forsaken me?"] cannot be a theoretical answer beginning with the word "Because." It has to be a practical answer. An experience of this kind can only be answered by another experience, not by an explanation.

Christ's question was answered, three days later, with resurrection. Not an explanation, but an answering experience. And the answer to human suffering and my impassioned cry of "why?" is also not a theoretical explanation. It is an experience. It is a relationship. Job asked why, and God didn't answer. Habakkuk asked why, and God didn't answer. God says in his silence: answers won't satisfy you. Only relationship can satisfy you.

I had asked God, way back in July, to teach me something about loving with my heart, not just with my mind and my will. I would not have guessed that God would answer by absconding, by silence. But after a semester of silence, I suddenly found I'd learned to love God.

I had to learn the feeling of God's absence to be able to recognize and appreciate his presence. I had to be a faithless servant before I could believe that God's love for me was not predicated on my usefulness to him. I had to learn that answers didn't satisfy before I could experience the relationship that does. I had to hate God's sovereignty before I could rejoice in it. I had to see God as wholly transcendent and wholly-other, beyond my ability to comprehend, before I could hear him chuckling in the dark.

And now I did hear his delightful and infuriating laughter; and now I did see his direct supply of all my needs.

I lingered in Gethsemane that Easter because for the first time I had tasted a drop of Christ's suffering, just a fragment of the forsakenness that Christ felt.

"Becoming like him in his death"—this might mean, in part, experiencing the suffering that is divine silence. And just as Christ's self-surrender led to the answering experience of resurrection, it is in our self-surrender—the final, exhausted, empty recognition that we have nothing to bring to God—that he begins to answer by bringing something to us. He gives himself.

Without realizing it, I had come to exactly the same conclusion that Elisabeth Elliot came to when she considered her first year of overseas work. She had spent a year in a jungle village, studying the local language and creating a written form of it so the Bible could be translated. Near the end of the year, one of her local friends died a seemingly meaningless death. Then, on the train home, her luggage, containing every bit of her translation work, was lost forever. She wrote:

> Each separate experience of individual stripping we may learn to accept as a fragment of the suffering Christ bore when he took it all. "Surely he hath borne our griefs and carried our sorrows." This grief, this sorrow, this total loss that empties my hands and breaks my heart, I may, if I will, accept, and by accepting it, I find in my hands something to offer. And so I give it back to him, who in mysterious exchange gives himself to me.

I lingered in Gethsemane in glad surrender to the silence of God, the absence of explanation, the answer of relationship.

Interlude

THE MISSIONARY

Why are we not all devoted to God; breathing the whole spirit of Missionaries?

John Wesley

Mission is putting love where love is not.

Attributed to St. John of the Cross

It may be time to retire the word.

Missionary was first used in the English language in 1625 by Edward Chaloner, a clergyman in the Church of England. He was a preacher, a writer, and academic. In his work, you find nuanced arguments and a careful attention to words. One of the big questions of his day, for example, was whether the Church of England had been born from the Roman Catholic church, or had originated separately. Chaloner said that it wasn't an either/or question: the Church of England in its earliest days consisted of reformers who had broken all ties with the Catholic church as well as all who kept in their hearts the simple faith of the early church, whatever denomination they found themselves in. Chaloner valued all truth, staying up to date on scientific developments, quoting ancient philosophers and poets, and studying Roman Catholic theology.

It's no surprise that a guy who loved language and the church so much would be the one to introduce the English term *missionary*, borrowed probably from French (*missionnaire*) or Spanish (*misionero*). He died of the plague at age thirty-four, the same year he wrote about Jesuit missionaries.

I have to wonder what Chaloner, with his love of precision and care for words, would think of the way this word has evolved in the four hundred years since his death.

In the beginning, *missionary* had a limited meaning: a celibate male, probably in a Catholic order, probably European, who had made a life commitment to evangelism.

But almost immediately that definition was complicated by the association of Catholic missionary orders with political colonization. The expansion of God's kingdom was in many ways conflated with the expansion of territory controlled by Catholic kings, and their quest to acquire land, labor, and raw materials.

The Protestant missionary movement did little to improve the associations. While Catholic missions had been inextricably bound to political expansion, American Protestant missions were born entwined with corporate-style capitalism. The first missionary boards were structured after secular trading societies, and their values were efficiency, production, and numbers-based assessments.

The word *missionary*, then, was born into the English language already weighted down with imperialist and capitalist baggage. It evolved and lost some of the negatives, though it would never shake them entirely, which is part of the reason people still give you the side-eye if you say you're a missionary.

The definition changed in some important ways, though, over the next couple of centuries: now the (imperialist, capitalist) missionary was not necessarily a celibate male committed for life; the missionary could be married, could be non-western, could be a woman!

And then somewhere around the late 1800s or early 1900s the word acquired a new set of connotations. Now missionaries were God's Special Forces. They were adventure heroes and "grabbers of the impossible," those who gave up "small ambitions" and went where the "real action" was. And this posed a new set of very current problems for the word.

The missionary vocation was marketed to a generation of us as the most spiritual vocation. We read biographies that were "high adventure as unreal as any successful novel," in the words of missionary Nate Saint. Amy Carmichael told us that "God's true missionary is a Nazarite, who has 'made a special vow, the vow of one separated, to separate himself unto the Lord.'" We began to believe that there were "holy" jobs and "ordinary" jobs, that some callings were simply more spiritual. And the music on the video or the conference stage crescendoed while a voice asked us to *go*, and we felt in our hearts that to *go* was always more noble than to stay.

The problem is that we went, and it wasn't all high adventure. Or we went, and we developed overinflated senses of our own spiritual importance. Or

we went, but we were unprepared for the realities of cross-cultural work, ill-equipped to serve in meaningful ways.

The problem is that we didn't go, but we believed the fact that we stayed made us second-class Christians. We stayed, so we thought that we were not called to evangelism like the *missionaries* were.

No vocation is more spiritual than another. And every Christian is called to share the gospel. But the very existence of the word *missionary* as it is used today seems to imply otherwise. If missionaries are God's Special Forces, then evangelism is a calling for some, for the super-spiritual. The rest of us just aren't called to that.

• • •

The word *missionary* has become more problematic than helpful. Instead of describing reality, it blurs our vision and limits our imaginations. It has outlived its usefulness, and I vote we give it a proper burial.

We need new ways of talking about God's work in the world. It's true that God is "on mission" to reveal his glory and love to all nations by spreading his kingdom on earth, and that we are to join in that mission, all of us. But God's mission has never been about counting the number of spiritual conversations you've had in a week or valuing street evangelism over changing diapers and formatting spreadsheets. God's mission has never been about seeing yourself as a spiritual superhero in an action story. God's mission, as St. John of the Cross said, is to put love where love is not. It's about relational flourishing.

We all share this vocation, but we live into it in different ways. Maybe your way is through cross-cultural evangelism. Maybe it's to be a first-grade teacher. Maybe it's to be a linguist and a Bible translator. Maybe it's to be a stay-at-home dad. Maybe it's to be a doctor in the suburbs, the inner city, or an African village. I don't know, but what I do know is that all of those vocations are valuable, and in all of those vocations, you can put love where love is not.

30

· · · · ·

Speaking Faith as a
Second Language

During my first year teaching overseas, I felt my ability to speak eloquently (or even articulately) in English slipping away from me. Most of my conversations used only the same, simple hundred words or so—whatever I said was stumbling, stilted, reliant upon body language, context, and tone to actually communicate meaning. It worried me: my neural pathways for language were overgrown with weeds, and for a writer, that's kind of a serious problem.

At some point, though, I began to appreciate what happened when communication was reduced to the lowest common denominator. We didn't hide behind fancy words anymore. Beauty existed in that simplicity; we agreed on the most basic of things, and didn't have to push beyond them. When words failed us, we took action. When my electric motorbike ran out of battery power on a lonely stretch of rice field, a pregnant woman had plugged in my bike and chopped open a coconut for me, patting me on the arm and handing me a drink when our ability to communicate with language ended.

Soon, too, I began to hear the poetry of words I had grown up with arranged in new ways, strange and lovely ways from both clumsy and careful language-learners' lips.

When Elisha was trying to recall a phrase he had read, he stopped me after class. "It's a locution," he told me, "a locution your grandparents might have used."

I raised my eyebrows. "You mean it's an old phrase?" I asked.

"Yes!" he said. "The phrase is 'low and . . .' something."

"Lo and behold," I guessed. His face lit up.

"That's it!" he cried. "I love it. It is so beautiful."

As I taught English as a second language, the beauty of our "locution" became ever new for me. I listened fascinated as my students used unique sentence constructions or outdated vocabulary words, unwittingly assigning new depth or stronger meaning to them by their new context. I fell in love with language all over again.

"I've received your e-mail," Avril wrote to me in my second year of teaching, "and I'm very cheerful to hear that you've organized Thanksgiving. It was jolly, wasn't it? I wanna send you my regard. . . . I imagine there is snow in the US now and there are many animated Christmas activities."

What native speaker would have called my Thanksgiving "jolly" and my Christmas activities "animated"? And yet, what better way could there have been to describe them? What better holiday gift to receive than a student's "regard"?

I had discovered one of the enduringly lovely gifts about teaching English to language learners: their speech makes old, tired words suddenly new and full of possibility. Somehow the grammatically incorrect structures open up the poetic meaning of the words; a surprising word choice can enhance the message rather than distract from it.

I was also learning that English—though my native language and one of the great loves of my life—didn't belong to me. It didn't belong to me, or to America, or to England, or to native speakers anywhere. As a language, English is a tool—not to be wielded in domination or colonialism, but used for negotiating meaning. Together. Limiting my language and hearing it in new contexts, in unexpected ways, even in grammatically incorrect ways, had actually expanded my love for it.

But the transformation of my English forced me to realize something even more important: my understanding of the language of faith needed to undergo the same kind of deconstruction and reconstruction for me to love it and use it rightly.

I used to think that I spoke "Christian" as a native language—that it belonged to me. I was born into a Christian-speaking family, and I "asked Jesus into my heart" practically as soon as I could form a sentence. I memorized

creeds, catechisms, and large portions of the Bible; I sang hymns by heart and praise choruses with hand-motions. As a native speaker, I trusted my comprehension of the language and doubted the legitimacy of anybody who understood the words differently than I did.

But in my second decade of fluency in the language of faith, I found that the words were stale. Familiarity with the Bible had dulled my perceptions, and the deepest truths had become tired clichés to my evangelical ears. I needed the language to become new for me just as English had, or I was in danger of losing it altogether. I needed to find people who spoke this language differently than I did, people who could help me find new ways into the well-worn truths I wanted to hold on to.

Reading Bible stories with people who had literally never heard of Moses, Esther, Mary, or Paul made them new for me. Simply hearing the words of Scripture in the new context of Southeast Asia gave them fresh meaning. Before that, I sort of understood what it meant for Jesus to be "the bread of life." But not until I lived in a place where every meal began with a bite of rice to honor the food that brought ancestors through famine, where every meal relied on rice (and, for many of my students, was little more than rice), where "how are you" translated literally as "have you eaten rice yet?" did I begin to comprehend what it meant for Jesus to be the bread of life. Here, he was the rice of life.

But it wasn't just those who had never heard the stories, or those from a different culture, that I needed. I realized I needed those who had grown up speaking the language but using the words differently than I did. Take prayer, for instance. Where I grew up, prayer was ACTS: Adoration, Confession, Thanksgiving, and Supplication. It was individual, personal, disembodied, methodical, and conversational.

After two decades of ACTS, I needed to learn about prayer from the Catholic church, where it was something communal and liturgical and sensual. I needed to learn about prayer from the desert fathers and mothers, where it was constant, a way of life, and bound up with mundane tasks like weaving and gardening. I needed charismatics to share their new languages with me, to help me become open to emotion and the power of the Holy Spirit in my life. I needed to learn about meditation from Buddhists, and to learn from Muslims how posture and practice affect prayer.

Putting *prayer* in any of those new contexts gave the word fresh meaning, enriching both my language and my faith.

I had long been the girl with the answers, the girl with the most verses memorized, the girl with the theological arguments well-honed, the one who

raised her hand first. But living cross-culturally had made me question all my assumptions. As I emerged from the dark night of the soul I'd experienced in Cambodia, I was less likely to try to put my beliefs into words. I was less likely to offer the right answer, and more likely to listen to what might be wrong answers, to see what I could learn from them.

When my card-house construction of God collapsed, and I began to see that he was farther beyond my understanding than I had ever realized, I was actually joining a long history of Christians who celebrated the inscrutability of the divine. I had begun to learn what Christians had always known: that God cannot be captured with words. When ancient and medieval writers tried to explain the impossibility of saying something true about God, they often quoted Psalm 116:11: *omnis homo mendax*. Everyone is a liar. Augustine, persistently worried over language, lamented the fact that there was no way of speaking and writing about God that was completely true. Martin Luther expressed the same idea in his Christmas Day sermon in 1522, when in the middle of exposition, he stopped and said:

> You see from this babbling of mine the immeasurable difference between the word of God and all human words, and how no man can adequately reach and explain a single word of God with all his words. It is an eternal word and must be understood and contemplated with a quiet mind.

I, who had been raised to "always be prepared to give an answer to everyone who asks you to give the reason for the hope that you have" (1 Peter 3:15), had fewer and fewer answers to give. I was more likely to preface my answers with an honest "I'm not sure, but maybe it's something like this."

Letting go of my ownership of the language of faith was sometimes frightening, unmooring. Instead of being the person with the answers, I became a person with questions. Instead of colonizing, I worked to cooperate. But in seeking to agree on the most basic of things, like the meaning of the word *prayer*, I found a simplicity of language which lent itself to coordinated action. My words took on gestures, form, and meaning in the real world.

Letting go of my ownership of the language of faith meant recognizing that I could only speak it as a second, and learned, language. The words of faith didn't belong to me, or to anyone but God, who was himself the Word made flesh. It was in this recognition that the language of faith was transformed for me, and it was in this that I, too, was transformed.

Epilogue

NO LONGER AT EASE

After dinner, Jack and I locked our five hundred-square-foot apartment and walked down the hill. The sky was pink, and the October air still warm; we were in the South, where "muggy" is the best description of the weather for at least six months out of twelve. The year we'd spent dating in Southern California had spoiled me, and I was always looking for moments that felt like Los Angeles did, all sunlight and 72, all beauty and color and yearning. Jack had proposed to me on a beach in Santa Barbara, and after the wedding in Little Rock we stayed in Arkansas, living near my family while we tried to figure out what to do next.

Ambitions had paled beside our need to simply be together, but now that we were, I struggled to know what my vocation was and how to live a meaningful life in the States. We weren't rich by American standards, but we had more than enough, and we were surrounded by people who looked like us: privileged, white Americans who could hear the gospel at one of the dozens of churches within a fifteen-mile radius. Our life together in Arkansas was beautiful and comfortable; and so, of course, I was conflicted about it. It was hard to feel like what we were doing was important.

I was working at a private high school as a librarian and teacher, and slowly reading N. T. Wright's *Surprised by Hope*. As Jack and I walked, I tried to describe the way the book was altering my understanding of what it meant to live a Christian life.

"I just can't believe, sometimes, that teaching these rich white kids about essay construction or the imagery in *The Giver* is meaningful. I mean, they already have everything they need, in abundance. They don't need me. How can this be as important as teaching the Bible in Southeast Asia, or even teaching English there, to students who really needed it to have viable career options?"

Unconsciously, I sped up as I spoke, my internal struggle punctuated by the slap of my footsteps on asphalt.

"You don't really believe that, though, do you?" Jack asked.

"I don't know. I feel it," I said, slowing down as we rounded a corner out of the neighborhood and toward our closest grocery store, the Fresh Market.

I paused to try to express the thought more clearly.

"People in church used to say, 'Only two things will last: the word of God and the souls of men,'" I began. "But that's not in the Bible. The Bible says *all* things will be made new. That Jesus is coming back here, to stay, to bring the fullness of the kingdom that he ushered in when he first came, to build the new heavens and the new earth here.

"If that's true," I continued, "then everything matters, not just evangelism. Any way in which we are helping to usher in Christ's kingdom matters. Any way we can find to contribute to making things new, to mending what is broken or healing what is sick or bringing wholeness to what is torn apart is kingdom work of value. There's no hierarchy of vocation."

Jack nodded. We stood in front of the freezer case, surveying an array of mostly small-batch, organic, locally made ice creams, each of which cost more than almost every meal I'd ever eaten overseas. "Do you want Häagen Dazs?" he asked.

"Is that even a question?" I said, grabbing a pint of chocolate peanut butter. We took it with two plastic spoons to a park bench outside the store.

"So working with these privileged kids isn't less important than working in Southeast Asia," Jack prompted.

"Maybe. If I can help Nathan understand his identity while his parents are divorcing, or help Hannah develop a healthy body image and relationship with food—then I'm helping to repair the broken world. I'm ushering in the promised Kingdom. Even washing dishes, or mending clothes, or planting a garden—even these tasks are Kingdom work. Cleaning the kitchen brings order to chaos. Altering hand-me-downs brings new purpose to something discarded as worthless. Weeding a vegetable garden nourishes new life."

"I guess I should read the book," he said, and I smiled.

It was hard to believe that small things done with love could be enough. I knew that I was beloved apart from my performance or my usefulness, but

I also knew that I could never be fully at peace while others suffered. How could I celebrate the good and the beautiful without giving up on the fight to right injustices? How could I rest in my status as the beloved of God without becoming complacent about the work that still needed to be done? How could I give up my savior complex without also giving up?

We climbed the hill back to our apartment as the sun set. Those are the kinds of questions you just have to live with.

• • •

With a new name and a new passport, I made it back into the country. I hadn't been sure it would work. When the organization called and asked if Jack and I would lead a team of American college students in conducting a summer English camp at a high school in the capital, we explained my situation. They said it was worth a try.

And I made it without even a hiccup through customs, back to the heat and the rice fields and the motorbikes and bowls of noodles fragrant with mint and cilantro. Our team stayed for a month in a hotel on a busy city street, walking to the high school to teach English courses every morning and afternoon, and to lead "cultural presentations" every evening. I tried to appreciate every moment we had there, not letting any detail of the experience pass me by: the sweat trickling down my back at seven in the morning, the huge iron wheelbarrows, women in pajamas sweeping the street with straw brooms, barefoot girls in traditional pink dresses slipping under a locked gate, a small beggar boy holding a cup and knocking at the café window, wooden sandals lined neatly outside the temple door.

In the off hours, Jack and I met with the American college students on our team, counseling them and offering training and support through their culture shock and first classroom experiences.

But again and again the experience disappointed me, beginning at team leader training, where the organization had prepared materials for Jack but not for me. They'd somehow forgotten I existed, not even assigning me a room. He was the team leader; I was a wife. I'd gotten over that hurt, just as I'd faced my fears of being turned away at the border. But spending a month leading an English camp, Jack and I found, was nothing like our previous experience; it was nothing like making a home in a foreign culture. Our responsibilities at the school kept us so busy that we rarely got to spend any time with students or other locals. All day, we taught English and American culture, never getting to really experience the Asian culture we'd grown to love.

Not every part of the trip was bad. I reconnected with Camille, befriended high school students who would one day come to college in the States, and prayed for the country's future. We even celebrated our one-year wedding anniversary with a quick night away. But the true highlight of the month was probably the night Jack and I had a long dinner with a student and her family in her home.

We'd simply wanted to enjoy the local culture, the slow pace of life, the deep relationships. Instead, the frantic activity of English camp drained us and the focus on teaching American culture made us sad. Some of the college students we worked with had emotional needs that we weren't equipped to meet, and trying to serve them exhausted our energy. Because our English camp students were so young, their parents didn't allow them to spend free hours with us, so our opportunities for building relationships were limited.

I knew all along it would be unwise for me to revisit the city where I'd lived, but I hoped maybe Veronica could meet me in the capital. Though our contact over the previous three years had been rare, I e-mailed her nearly as soon as we landed. I was around—would she be able to meet? She responded quickly. She would take the train.

But the next day, she contacted me again. The police had "happened" to drop by for a visit shortly after she'd e-mailed me, she said; her parents didn't think it was a good idea for her to come to the capital. Of course they were right, but it baffled me. It had been three full years since the police had first questioned Veronica about her beliefs. Were they really still reading her e-mails?

Guilt like a gut punch, again. Had I done more harm than good? Had I made Veronica's life better, or worse? Had I ruined her relationships with her best friends? Had I put her family in continual danger? Did she have any job prospects, or would she always be on the outside of her community, thanks to me?

Why did new life have to feel so much like death?

A few months after the trip, I would pose those questions to Lisa, and her answers would be swift and certain: What you did was good, she'd say. You brought salvation to her. She knows God because of you.

I hope so.

But years out, I have no way of knowing if Veronica is parched or flourishing. All I can do is trust that God does love her, more than I do, and that God will never leave her or forsake her.

• • •

So what will I tell them, these American college students who have fallen in love with the country during our month here, and are thinking of returning to Asia for longer periods of time?

I'll tell them that cross-cultural exchange is far more complicated than I understood when I first moved to Southeast Asia, but that this isn't cause for despair. This isn't a reason not to go. Instead, it's a reason for those who go to stay longer, to be more curious, to seek partnerships and reciprocal relationships, to always maintain the posture of a learner.

I'll tell them that cross-cultural exchange is far more shattering than I had ever expected. My understandings of God, faith, heroism, sacrifice, and surrender fell to pieces while I was overseas. I realized just how much of my understanding of Christianity was cultural rather than essential. I realized how little I knew. Rebuilding my language of faith became a lifelong—and life-giving—work.

It's all been more heart-wrenching and more beautiful than I could ever have guessed it would be.

Being one of "heaven's heroes" has very little to do with high adventure—persecution is not glamorous. It's not about wanderlust or never being "bored." It doesn't even have much to do with the passion of my commitment to Christ.

But understanding what it means to be held by God, to be beloved apart from performance, is the heart of the gospel. Ironically, I wasn't really able to grasp that truth until I went to share it in another country.

Some of these American college students will talk to me about calling. They will wonder if their vocations lie overseas. And this is what I'll say: "calling" is a complicated beast. If you want to go, you should go, but only in full recognition of your status as the Beloved of God, in full recognition of your own mixed motives, your very limited understanding of any situation, your need to be a learner. Don't go out of guilt or desire to achieve. Don't go because you want to be one of heaven's heroes. Don't go to save the world—go because you want to learn to love it. Go because you know that you are loved.

You are loved, you are loved, you are loved.

Further Reading

I grew up reading missionary biographies, and as I wrote this book I re-read some of those and devoured many more, as well as several books on missiology. For shaping the ideas I present in the Interludes, I am particularly indebted to:

Short-Term Mission: An Ethnography of Christian Travel Narrative and Experience by **Brian Howell**

There is no shortage of books critiquing short-term mission trips, but Howell's approach to the topic is unique. As an anthropologist and a Christian, he studies the phenomenon of the short-term trip in a way that is both academic and personal. In this book you'll get a brief history of the short-term mission trip, as well as a close look at the narratives we use to talk about our trips—and why those narratives matter.

Playing God: Redeeming the Gift of Power by **Andy Crouch**

We've been given power and privilege, but what are we to do with it—particularly with regard to the work of evangelism and the fight for justice? Crouch's answers are intriguing, especially in his chapter on injustice. He argues that American Christians often act like "little gods" on short-term mission trips, and he advocates a change in approach.

Overturning Tables: Freeing Missions from the Christian-Industrial Complex by **Scott Bessenecker**

Through research and story, Bessenecker shows that many of our Christian "ministries" have been shaped more by the values of the free market than

by the values of the kingdom of God. Our metrics of success in mission are borrowed from the corporate world rather than taken from Scripture. How can we change? Bessenecker has some ideas worth exploring.

Red, Brown, Yellow, Black, White—Who's More Precious in God's Sight? A Call for Diversity in Christian Missions and Ministry by Leroy Barber with Velma Maia Thomas

To be honest, I never wondered why missionaries from America were predominantly white until I started researching for this book. Leroy Barber explains why and how our missionary organizations are structured to benefit white people and disadvantage people of color, and offers some helpful directions forward.

Guardians of the Great Commission: The Story of Women in Modern Missions by Ruth Tucker

I can't even imagine the amount of research that went into the writing of this masterful history of women in missions. Abundantly readable, quietly subversive, and skillfully woven together, this book ought to be read by anyone seeking to understand the nineteenth- and twentieth-century missionary movements.

Other sources

For more on the early nineteenth-century missionary movement, the best resources I found were in academic journals. Two particularly helpful articles are "David Brainerd and the Nineteenth Century Missionary Movement" by Joseph Conforti in the *Journal of the Early Republic* and "Can Women Be Missionaries? Envisioning Female Agency in the Early Nineteenth-Century British Empire" by Clare Midgley in the *Journal of British Studies.*

Acknowledgments

Many thanks to my agent, Heidi Mitchell, for taking a chance on me. I'm indebted to my editor, Miranda Gardner, and the entire team at Discovery House, especially Paul Muckley and Andy Rogers. You made the publishing process a joy.

Thanks to *The Curator* for publishing the original version of the essay "Speaking Faith as a Second Language," which appears slightly edited in this book.

I'm grateful to early readers who offered helpful feedback, particularly Katie Glupker, Meredith Pace, Lauren Winner, Briana Meade, Elizabeth Ann Lepine, Julia Oller, and Kirsten Kosik.

Collegeville Institute, Taylor University's BCTLE, Shepherd's Gate Inn, and The Bridge: thank you for precious gifts of time in quiet places of beauty.

Katie and Elliott Walker offered the best of Brooklyn hospitality and one of the first places where I could get away to focus on this book. Katie, thank you for often being my first and best reader.

Beth and Dan Bowman: you are the kinds of friends who help me believe that all things are possible. Here's to many more nights on the back porch.

Thanks to Anna and Mollie for lifelong friendship that sometimes understands me better than I understand myself.

I might never have written this book if it weren't for Danielle Mayfield, Jessica Goudeau, Kelley Nikondeha, Christiana Peterson, and Stina Kielsmeier-Cook. For your activist pushes, your academic smarts, your theological brilliance, your mystic hearts, your astute edits, and your support, friendship, laughter, tears, chickens, and monkey business, I am forever grateful.

Katie, Jimmy, John, and David, you are all the GOAT. Thanks for being first readers and for making life so good.

I'm able to believe that God is good and that God is love because of the way my parents have loved me. Mom, Dad, *thank you* is inadequate. But thank you.

Rosie and Owen—why do I write like I'm running out of time? In part, to be sure that you will have these stories forever. Sorry about all the movies you had to watch while I was writing.

And most of all, of course, Jack: words fail. Thank you for your patience and grace, for the hours you spent with the kids while I wrote, for your thoughtful notes on the manuscript, for your gentle wisdom. You make me better. I love you.

About the Author

Amy Peterson teaches and works with the Honors program at Taylor University. With a B.A. in English Literature from Texas A&M and an M.A. in Intercultural Studies from Wheaton College, Amy taught ESL for two years in Southeast Asia before returning stateside to teach in California, Arkansas, and Washington. Amy is a regular contributor to *Our Daily Bread* and *Off the Page*. She has written for *Books & Culture*, *Christianity Today*, *The Other Journal*, *Comment Magazine*, *The Cresset*, *The Living Church*, and *Art House America*, among other places.

Read more of Amy's writing on her blog, amypeterson.net, and sign up for her newsletter to receive giveaways, book and blog recommendations, and links to the best of her published writing.

twitter.com/amylpeterson
instagram.com/amypete
pinterest.com/amypete

Enjoy this book?
Help us get the word out!

- Share a link to the book or mention it on social media.
- Write a review on your blog, on a retailer site, or on our website (dhp.org).
- Pick up another copy to share with someone.
- Recommend this book for your church, book club, or small group.
- Follow Discovery House on social media and join the discussion.

Contact us to share your thoughts:

Discovery House
P.O. Box 3566
Grand Rapids, MI 49501 USA
Call: 1-800-653-8333
Email: books@dhp.org
Website: dhp.org

"We all love a good story. You know, where the practically perfect hero overcomes obstacles to accomplish a great feat, but is terribly maligned in the process, yet is vindicated in the end, and everyone lives happily ever after. But this is not that story. Amy Peterson's *Dangerous Territory* is too honest to indulge the hero façade and too authentic to avoid the unresolved questions. But real stories are like that. If you want to read a real story, a well-told story, a story where shallow Christian missionary triumphalism is replaced by the messy, unresolved, and sometimes tragic life of faith, then read this story. In *Dangerous Territory* we set aside our adolescent faith with its tidy answers and clean endings, and we take up an adult faith; a faith with real risk, real loss, real questions, and God's presence on the other side of pain."

Scott Bessenecker, author and interim director of missions,
InterVarsity Christian Fellowship

"There is a disarming determination in these pages not to let Christian faith go until its blessings are known and felt."

Wesley Hill, author of *Spiritual Friendship* and Assistant Professor of
Biblical Studies, Trinity School for Ministry

"Missionary work is wrapped in mystique. It may be vilified as the remnants of colonialism and imperialism, or held up as the highest calling the Christian can obtain. The reality is that it is life—messy, real life. In this book Amy Peterson opens up her messy, ordinary, and beautiful life to let us see what it meant for her to go from a young woman wrapped in the mythology of missionary heroes, through dark days of disillusionment, into a deeper, more grounded understanding of faith and calling. Along the way, she mixes in history, analysis, and thoughtful reflection. This genre-bending book is a delightful addition to memoirs of mission that gives us a personal and honest picture of a missionary life on the way."

Brian M. Howell, Professor of Anthropology, Wheaton College

"Amy's is a story of a life broken open and
We need more brave stories like hers."

A Story of Q

"Peterson's thoughtful and vulnerable exploration of her missionary experiences urges us to peel away the layers. To learn, finally, what it is to rest in our own Belovedness."

Addie Zierman, author of *Night Driving* and *When We Were on Fire*

"People are both hungry to hear stories of what God is up to all over the world and uneasy at how these stories have traditionally been told. This is why *Dangerous Territory* is a must-read for anyone, like myself, who longs to be a part of the global story of God's coming kingdom. Here, Peterson unpacks the layers of the traditional missionary narrative in ways that are subversive, profound, and ultimately hopeful."

D. L. Mayfield, author of *Assimilate or Go Home:
Notes from a Failed Missionary on Rediscovering Faith*

"Amy Peterson describes how the idealized Christianity of her youth was confronted by a complicated world. Faith and doubt are revealed to be conversation partners, and God's love and presence is found in the midst of both. Her writing is vulnerable and beautiful, and she is a good companion for Christians in search of an earthy, ordinary faith."

Michael Cosper, founder and director of Harbor Media

"Do not read this book if you are content with safe categories, messiah complexes, or serving God as a way to serve yourself. Do read this book if you want to wrestle with a God who works outside our boxes and humbles us in the process. By sharing so freely from her own life, Peterson gives us the opportunity to invite His work into ours. Simultaneously devastating and comforting, *Dangerous Territory* calls us beyond our simplistic notions of commitment to God to a place of full surrender."

Hannah Anderson, author of *Humble Roots:
How Humility Grounds and Nourishes Your Soul*